GREAT GIANTS STORIES

Every Young Fan Should Know

Second Edition

Julie and Scott Jackson

Illustrations by Johnny Hansell

ISBN-13: 978-0-9891497-0-9
ISBN-10: 0-9891497-0-6

To Ben and Amanda,
and young fans everywhere.

CONTENTS

Introduction   i

How the Giants Got Their Name   1

Baseball's Odd Couple: McGraw and Mathewson   4

Memphis Bill, Master Melvin, and the Meal Ticket   13

The Shot Heard 'Round the World   20

Willie Mays: The Five-Tool Player   27

Going, Going, Gone   37

New Hometown Heroes   42

Life at the 'Stick   48

1962: The Best Ever?   54

Marichal vs. Spahn   63

Spitballs and a Moon Shot   68

Dave Dravecky's Miracle Comeback   72

Earthquake!   78

Splash Hit: A New Ballpark in China Basin   87

Following in Giant Footsteps   94

Near Misses   102

Torture   111

Back From the Brink   126

INTRODUCTION

SINCE THE VERY BEGINNING, baseball and storytelling have gone hand in hand. And the Giants baseball club—with its rich history of colorful characters, epic battles, and dramatic victories—has produced some of the very best sports stories of all time.

Whether you're a young Giants fan or just young at heart, these are the stories you need to know, the ones that will continue to be passed down from each generation of Giants fans to the next.

As you read, you'll go all the way back to the team's early days in New York City, when baseball was brand new. You'll follow the team's move west and experience the many exciting moments the Giants brought to fans in San Francisco.

Along the way, you'll meet some of the game's greatest superstars as well as unexpected heroes. You'll discover thrilling tales of triumph but also tragic twists of fate. All of these together have made the Giants a fun and fascinating team throughout the years.

Once you know these stories, you'll be prouder than ever to call yourself a Giants fan.

HOW THE GIANTS GOT THEIR NAME

BACK IN THE "OLD DAYS," many baseball teams had names that sound funny to us now. In fact, in the very early years of professional baseball, most teams didn't have any nicknames at all. They simply took the name of the city or town where they played—the Chicagos, the Bostons, and so on.

Some teams started using nicknames based on the color of their uniforms. A few of those team names have lasted into the modern era, such as the Cincinnati Red Stockings (now just the Reds) and the Chicago White Stockings (today's White Sox). But there were others that have long disappeared—have you ever heard of the St. Louis Brown Stockings, the Milwaukee Grays, or the Hartford Dark Blues?

Sometimes sports reporters of the day would make

up their own nicknames for teams, and those names often changed from year to year. The Cleveland team was known for a while as the "Spiders" because a lot of their players had long arms and legs. The city of Boston was sometimes known as "Beantown," so for several years their baseball team was called the "Beaneaters." Imagine sitting in the stands and yelling, "GO, BEANEATERS!"

There was a team in Brooklyn, New York, that started out as the "Atlantics." Then, in one season, six players on the team got married, so they became known as the "Bridegrooms." Later, in the 1890s, the city of Brooklyn put in a new streetcar trolley system. People who lived there were called "trolley-dodgers" because they had to get out of the way of the new trolley cars barreling down the crowded streets. The local team thus became the "Brooklyn Trolley Dodgers." Does that name sound a little familiar? The trolleys are long since gone, and the "Dodgers" no longer play in Brooklyn, but they've kept their name—and their bitter rivalry with the Giants— for more than a hundred years.

As for the Giants themselves, the team was formed in New York in 1883. At first they weren't very creative with their name: they were just the "New Yorks." Sometimes they were called the "Gothams," because Gotham was often used as another name for New York City.

Then, one day in 1885, the Gothams won a thrilling game in extra innings. When their proud manager, Jim Mutrie, met with reporters after the game, he affectionately referred to his players as "My big fellows! My *giants*!"

The name stuck, and "Giants" soon became the official team name.

Good thing he didn't call them his "snoogly-woogums," huh?

BASEBALL'S ODD COUPLE: McGRAW AND MATHEWSON

BASEBALL, LIKE MOST SPORTS, brings together players of different backgrounds, cultures, and personalities. Sometimes this can lead to some unusual and surprising friendships, and there are "odd couples" scattered throughout the history of baseball. But perhaps the most strangely successful of them all was the unlikely combination of John McGraw and Christy Mathewson.

John McGraw was a scrawny but tough Irish kid who grew up in New York. He was an excellent ball-player, and he became the leading star of the Baltimore Orioles in the 1890s. The Orioles were notorious at the time for their very aggressive play, which is a nice way of saying they played "dirty." As the Orioles' third baseman, McGraw would do whatever it took to slow

4

down a runner—block him, trip him, spike him, or even grab his belt loop as he tried to round the base! In those days there was only one umpire, and he had to watch the path of the ball, so McGraw and his teammates often got away with these kinds of shenanigans.

As you might expect, opposing teams didn't appreciate the rough play, and there were often fights on the field or after the games. Most of the time, McGraw would be right in the middle of those fights. One coach reportedly said that McGraw "eats gunpowder every morning and washes it down with warm blood." He probably wasn't the kind of guy your mom and dad would want you hanging around with!

Although McGraw, or "Muggsy," was despised by many people (especially umpires!), nobody could deny his talent. As a player he led the Orioles to three consecutive championships in 1894, 1895, and 1896. He and his teammates helped to develop new strategies that are still used by players today, like the hit-and-run and the squeeze play. They became famous for the "Baltimore chop," where the batter "chops" down on top of the ball to make it bounce high off the hard ground in front of the plate, giving him enough time to run to first.

McGraw excelled at all these tricks and more, but he was a great hitter as well. His career on-base percentage was a remarkable .466, which still ranks third all-time, behind only Ted Williams and Babe Ruth. That's some pretty impressive company!

By 1902, McGraw's career as a player was mostly finished, and New York owner John Brush hired him mid-season to manage his struggling Giants. The team definitely needed some help. They were suffering through a horrible year of 48 wins and 88 losses and eventually finished 53½ games out of first place. The New York players were eager for a change, but they were probably a little nervous about playing for this man who was so legendary for his fiery temper.

One Giants player at the time was a young right-handed pitcher named Christy Mathewson. He hadn't done that well as a pitcher in his first two seasons, and the previous manager thought he might be better playing in the infield. McGraw, however, thought that was a stupid idea, and he was never bashful about sharing his opinion. He had been in baseball long enough to know a good arm when he saw it, and under his guidance Mathewson quickly became the ace of the Giants' pitching staff.

Mathewson was the complete opposite of McGraw in almost every way. Standing next to the short, pot-bellied, pale-faced McGraw, Mathewson looked like the classic

"All-American" boy: tall, lean, and handsome, with golden hair and blue eyes. Unlike McGraw, who had survived a scrappy childhood on the tough streets of New York, Mathewson had grown up as the privileged son of a wealthy farmer in Pennsylvania. He had gone to college (which was rare for ballplayers in that day), where he was elected class president, sang in the glee club, and excelled in both football and baseball. He was popular and friendly and admired for his strong morals, "clean living," and good sportsmanship—quite a contrast to his new manager!

You might think that Mathewson, also known as "The Christian Gentleman," would have been reluctant to play for a rough man like McGraw. But in fact Mathewson had a lot of respect for McGraw's baseball talent and knowledge. To everyone's surprise, they soon became friends, and together they started making the Giants into winners.

As a manager, John McGraw wasn't very different than he had been as a player. He'd always do whatever it took to get a win. During games, he'd hurl insults at umpires, opposing players, and sometimes even his own players. He still got in fistfights, too, and he was kicked out of 131 games in his turbulent career.

McGraw ruled with such strict authority that he

became known as "Little Napoleon." He wanted things done his way and his way only. If players did something wrong, he'd slap them with a fine (or maybe just slap them, period).

McGraw was so obsessive about controlling the lives of his players that he even insisted on seeing their hotel dinner checks to be sure they weren't eating junk food or drinking alcohol. He was especially hard on one overweight catcher named Shanty Hogan. So Hogan made a deal with a waiter who would bring him apple pie à la mode for dessert—but write down "asparagus" on his bill instead!

As you might imagine, most of the Giants players didn't like McGraw much, but they did like playing for a winning team. And, under McGraw's leadership, the Giants started winning a lot.

Christy Mathewson was a huge part of that winning formula as he quickly established himself as one of the game's best pitchers and most popular players. He had a lively fastball and excellent control of his pitches. His secret weapon was the "fadeaway" pitch, which was a kind of reverse curve that broke sharply in on right-handed batters and "faded away" from the batter's line of sight (modern players call it a "screwball"). This pitch was very hard to hit and also hard to throw, since it required a strange twist of the forearm. Mathewson couldn't throw the pitch more than about ten times a game, but batters always had to be ready for it.

In 1904, just two years after McGraw took over as manager, the Giants posted a record 106 victories and easily won the National League pennant. However, McGraw and owner John Brush refused to have the Giants play against the winner of the American League in a championship series. The American League had only been around for two years, and McGraw considered it an inferior league. He thought his Giants were too good to play against the "junior circuit."

In 1905, the Giants had another outstanding year. Mathewson dominated the league, winning 31 games and posting an ERA of 1.28 as the team stormed to another NL pennant. This time, the team agreed to play the AL champion Philadelphia Athletics in a best-of-seven series, starting a chain of "World Series" contests that continues unbroken to this day.

And what a World Series it was—a true pitchers' duel with every game ending in a shutout. The Athletics had two future Hall of Fame hurlers in Eddie Plank and Chief Bender, but even they were no match for "Matty."

Mathewson pitched brilliantly in Game 1, allowing only four hits and no walks. He also helped himself at the plate by singling in the fifth inning and hitting a key sacrifice in the ninth. The Giants overcame Plank to win that first game, 3-0.

In Game 2, McGraw sent 21-game winner Joe McGinnity to the mound, and he gave up only six hits. Unfortunately, Chief Bender completely shut down the Giants' offense, and Philadelphia won 3-0 to even the series score at one game apiece.

McGraw turned to Mathewson again in Game 3. Even with only two days rest, his star pitcher did not disappoint. Again Mathewson allowed only four hits in the whole game. The Giants' offense was on fire, and New York romped to an easy 9-0 win.

Game 4 was yet another tense pitchers' duel as McGinnity and Plank took turns putting up zeroes on the scoreboard. It would take only one run to win it, and the Giants managed to score that run thanks partly to a Philadelphia error in the fourth inning. McGinnity held the A's hitters at bay the rest of the way, and the Giants won 1-0 to go up three games to one in the series.

It seems hard to imagine, but McGraw wanted Mathewson to pitch again in Game 5, even though he'd had only one day of rest and the Giants had other pitchers available. But McGraw liked to say, "The main idea is to win"—and nobody had done that for him more consistently than Christy Mathewson. So, for the third time in only six days, Mathewson took the mound. And, for the third time in only six days, he shut out the Athletics, allowing only six hits and no walks. The Giants managed just two runs against Bender, but it was enough to give them a 2-0 win and their first World Series victory.

Mathewson's mound work in the Series was truly remarkable. He pitched *three* complete-game shutouts. Some people say it was the greatest World Series performance ever by a single player.

Christy Mathewson went on to have many more great years for the Giants and became baseball's first national superstar. In today's game, a pitcher considers it a terrific season if he gets 20 or more wins. Mathewson did that twelve years in a row—and in four of those years he won 30 or more.

Mathewson was so admired that he was chosen as one of the first five players to be enshrined in the National Baseball Hall of Fame. His Cooperstown plaque reads simply: "MATTY WAS MASTER OF THEM ALL."

And John McGraw? He kept fighting—and kept winning. In his 31 years as the manager of the Giants, his teams finished in either first or second place 21 times. They won ten National League pennants and three World Series. His 2,840 wins as manager make him second all-time only to Connie Mack (who coincidentally was manager of the losing Athletics in that dramatic 1905 World Series). Mack himself once said, "There has been only one manager, and his name is John McGraw."

Together, this very odd couple of "Matty" and "Muggsy" made the Giants one of the greatest teams of the early 20th century. They certainly earned the honor of having their numbers retired by the Giants. But there's just one problem: players didn't even have numbers on their uniforms in those early days of baseball. So John McGraw and Christy Mathewson are immortalized in the Giants ballpark with two "NY" logos hanging side-by-side above the left field wall.

MEMPHIS BILL, MASTER MELVIN, AND THE MEAL TICKET

MAYS. MCCOVEY. MARICHAL. These are players that any diehard Giants fan knows. You may not have seen them play, but there's a good chance your parents or grandparents did, and they probably have wonderful stories to tell of watching these legends in action.

Terry. Ott. Hubbell. Those names are probably not quite so familiar to modern-day fans. But Bill Terry, Mel Ott, and Carl Hubbell were legendary in their time and are all in the Hall of Fame today. Together, they helped New York continue its winning legacy throughout the 1920s, 30s, and 40s.

These three great Giants never played for any other team, and they are among the select few to have their uniform numbers retired by the franchise.

Bill Terry (#3) was a left-handed first baseman who played for the Giants from 1923 to 1936. "Memphis Bill" was an excellent hitter who batted over .320 for nine years in a row. No left-handed hitter in the modern National League has ever had a higher career batting average than Terry's .341.

Bill Terry is best known for being the last NL batter to hit over .400 in a season. He accomplished the rare feat in 1930, when he tied the league record in total hits (254) and finished the year with a .401 batting average. He was so proud of that historic season that when asked for his autograph, he'd sign his name and scratch in ".401" below.

When John McGraw finally decided to retire in 1932, he asked Terry to take over as manager of the Giants. In those days it was not uncommon for active players to also be managers. So Terry continued to play first base while managing the ballclub. He proved to be good at both jobs and led the team all the way to a World Series victory over the Washington Senators in 1933.

The next year, a reporter asked him a question about his team's rivals, the Brooklyn Dodgers, who weren't playing very well at that time. In fact, the Dodgers were coming off a last-place season. Terry asked sarcastically, "Is Brooklyn still in the league?"

Though Terry meant it as a joke, the Dodgers didn't appreciate his sense of humor. They got the last laugh by beating the Giants in the last two games of the season to deny them the pennant. Despite that setback, the Giants and Bill Terry returned to take the National League pennants in 1936 and 1937. And "Memphis Bill" kept his jokes to himself after that.

Mel Ott (#4) played 22 seasons for the New York Giants, from 1926 to 1947. He was only 17 years old and fresh out of high school in Louisiana when he first tried out for the team. During tryouts, manager John McGraw was shocked by the youngster's unusual batting style. A left-handed hitter, Ott would raise his front (right) foot high in the air as the pitch was thrown and then plant it as he swung. It looked awkward, but McGraw noticed that it seemed to work—Ott was crushing the ball deep into the outfield.

McGraw didn't want any minor-league managers to mess around trying to "fix" that unusual swing, so he put the youngster on his own major league roster. Though Ott didn't get to play much in his first couple of years on the team, he sat next to McGraw on the bench and learned the game from the master. When Ott finally got to start in 1928, he soon showed that

McGraw's instincts had been right.

In 1929 Ott batted .328 and belted 42 home runs. A natural pull-hitter, he was helped by the odd shape of the Polo Grounds, which had a very short right field fence at only 258 feet. But Ott also hit plenty of homers in other ballparks. Probably the sweetest of all was the one he hit in the tenth inning of Game 5 to win the 1933 World Series. He finished his career in 1947 with 511 home runs, which at the time put him third on the all-time list behind only Babe Ruth and Jimmie Foxx.

More than just a powerful slugger with a funny leg kick, "Master Melvin" was also a solid right fielder and a popular player with his teammates and the New York fans. So when Bill Terry retired as manager in 1942, he passed the job down to Ott, who continued as a player/manager for several seasons.

Though well-liked and respected, Ott was not very successful as a manager. In fact, the Giants never finished higher than third under his leadership. When Leo Durocher, the hated manager of the rival Brooklyn Dodgers, said that "Nice guys finish last," he was talking about Mel Ott. Giants fans were outraged, but Durocher may have been right. The Giants didn't start winning again until they fired Mel Ott and hired a new manager: the much-despised Durocher himself.

Carl Hubbell (#11) was a left-handed pitcher for the New York Giants from 1928 to 1943. He is famous for his mastery of the baffling pitch known as the "screwball." This was the same kind of reverse curveball that Christy Mathewson called a "fadeaway." But while Mathewson only threw this tricky pitch a few times per game, Carl Hubbell made a living off the screwball. He threw it so many times that his left arm was permanently deformed. When his arm dangled at his side, it bent so that his palm faced outward.

But "King Carl" had a lot of success with his screwball, which he could control with almost perfect accuracy. In only his second year in the majors, he threw a no-hitter against the Pirates. In 1933, he pitched 18 scoreless innings and didn't give up a single walk in a 1-0 win over St. Louis. A few years later, he had an unprecedented streak of 24 straight victories, a major league record that still stands today.

Carl Hubbell was nicknamed "The Meal Ticket" by his fellow players because he was so reliable and consistent. They knew they could count on him, and he delivered many satisfying victories for the Giants and their fans, including two complete-game victories in the 1933 World Series.

However, the most memorable moment of Hubbell's

career came during the 1934 All-Star Game. This was only the second All-Star Game ever, but the Midsummer Classic was already a huge hit with the fans. More than 48,000 people packed into the stands at the Polo Grounds to see their favorite superstars from both leagues.

Hubbell was the obvious choice to start the game, but he got into some trouble early. He gave up a single to the leadoff hitter and then walked the second batter. With no outs and two men on, Hubbell must have swallowed hard as the next batter stepped up to the plate: a big fellow by the name of Babe Ruth.

Hubbell knew he'd have to rely on his screwball. He just hoped he could get the slugger to hit something on the ground. But Ruth looked completely baffled by Hubbell's "screwgie," which dipped sharply and seemed to slow down as it reached the plate. On just four pitches, Hubbell struck out the mighty Babe, who walked away shaking his head.

Next up to bat: Lou Gehrig, who was on his way to winning the Triple Crown that year as the league leader in batting average, home runs, and RBIs. "The Iron Horse" very rarely struck out. But Hubbell's signature pitch proved too much for him too, and Gehrig whiffed at a screwball below his knees for strike three.

Carl Hubbell still couldn't relax, though, for up next was Jimmie Foxx, the fearsome Philadelphia slugger known as "The Beast." But Hubbell stuck with that nasty screwball, and Foxx too went down swinging.

Just like that, Hubbell had gotten out of the first-inning jam. The crowd roared.

In the second inning, King Carl picked up right where he'd left off. He struck out both Al Simmons and Joe Cronin—two powerhouse hitters with lifetime batting averages over .300—before finally giving up a single. He got out of that jam too, and pitched another scoreless inning before leaving the game.

Once Hubbell was gone, the American League finally got some runs on the board, and they eventually ended up winning the 1934 All-Star Game. But what baseball fans everywhere still remember today is Hubbell's remarkable performance.

Though his career numbers make him one of the greatest Giant pitchers ever, Carl Hubbell will always be known as the man who once fanned five future Hall of Famers—all in a row.

THE SHOT HEARD 'ROUND THE WORLD

walk-off home run *n.* A home run in the bottom of the last inning that ends the game and causes the losing team to glumly walk off the field while the winners erupt in wild celebration.

THE TERM "WALK-OFF HOME RUN" is fairly new. But players have been hitting them—much to the delight of their fans—since the beginning of baseball. Some people think there's nothing more exciting in all of sports. And the most dramatic walk-off of them all was hit by Bobby Thomson of the New York Giants on October 3, 1951.

But what exactly made this particular home run so memorable? It wasn't a walk-off grand slam. It wasn't hit during a World Series game. And while Thomson was a good player who had a great season in 1951, he wasn't a superstar at the time and isn't in the Hall of Fame today.

It wasn't even a particularly monstrous home run—just a hard line drive that cleared the short left field fence. Why, then, do people still remember this as one of the greatest sports moments ever? To figure that out, we have to rewind the newsreel...

Go back to the middle of August 1951—the hot, humid "dog days" of summer in New York. Though there was a month and a half left in the regular baseball season, things looked hopeless for the Giants and their fans. Their hated archrivals, the Brooklyn Dodgers, were stampeding toward the pennant with a huge 13½ game lead over the second-place Giants. Now, a 13½ game lead that late in the season is as close to a sure thing as you can get. The Giants were really, truly, completely out of it.

Or so it seemed.

On August 12, something remarkable began. The Giants swept the Philadelphia Phillies in a double-header, and then they just kept on winning. In fact, they won 16 games in a row. The Dodgers, meanwhile, continued to play good baseball themselves, seemingly good enough to hold onto that enormous lead. But the Giants didn't let up.

The Giants' manager, Leo "The Lip" Durocher, had been fired by the Dodgers just a few years earlier, and you can figure he took particular pleasure in slowly whittling away at his old team's lead in the pennant race. With Durocher at the helm, the Giants played their best when it mattered most, and they finished the season with seven straight victories.

So, on the last day of the regular season, the pressure was all on Brooklyn. The Dodgers had to win their final game against Philadelphia just to stay alive. It was a taut battle, but when Brooklyn star Jackie Robinson finally launched the game-winning home run in the fourteenth inning, the Dodgers had clinched a tie with the Giants. Now the two teams would have to battle head-to-head in a three-game playoff to determine the National League champion.

The Giants' incredible comeback had dominated headlines for weeks, and New York City was electric with excitement as the playoff series got underway. You have to remember that this was (and still is) one of the most passionate, bitter rivalries in sports. If you were a Giants fan, you despised the Dodgers. If you were a Dodgers fan, you loathed the Giants. Tensions ran high as people from both sides packed the stands to cheer on their heroes.

The series kicked off at Brooklyn's Ebbetts Field, where the Giants took the first game of the series 3-1. The big blow came from Bobby Thomson, who swatted a two-run homer off Dodgers pitcher Ralph Branca in the fourth inning.

In Game 2, the Giants returned home to the Polo Grounds but were pounded by the Dodgers, 10-0. So the series was tied, and after six long months of baseball, it would come down to a single winner-take-all game for the National League pennant.

The entire nation would be watching. Game 3, played at the Polo Grounds, was the first baseball game broadcast nationwide on live television. Fans across the country tuned in to see how the exciting season-long drama would play out.

They would not be disappointed.

It was a pitching matchup of 20-game winners, with Sal "The Barber" Maglie starting for the Giants and Don Newcombe taking the mound for the Dodgers. Maglie gave up a quick run in the first inning, but after that both pitchers took turns hanging zeroes on the scoreboard. The Giants finally broke through in the seventh inning, when Bobby Thomson delivered a sacrifice fly to tie the game. But Thomson's day was far from over.

The Dodgers fought back with three runs in the eighth as Maglie began to tire, and Brooklyn had a 4-1 lead going into the bottom of the ninth inning. It seemed like the Giants' miracle comeback season might have finally run out of miracles.

Newcombe had to get only three more outs, but he was also getting tired. He gave up back-to-back singles to Alvin Dark and Don Mueller to start the ninth inning. After Monte Irvin popped up for the first out, Whitey Lockman doubled to left field, scoring Dark and closing the gap to 4-2.

But Don Mueller, running hard from first on that play, slid awkwardly into third base and broke his ankle. While he was being carried off the field, the Dodgers' manager, Charlie Dressen, decided Newcombe was done, and he brought in Ralph Branca, the Game 1 starter, to pitch to the next batter.

As you might have guessed, Bobby Thomson was the next batter. He felt terrible for his injured teammate. Still, Thomson had to focus on the game. The Giants were down two runs and had only two outs left, but they also had two runners in scoring position. He knew that a home run would win the game.

Manager Leo Durocher pulled Thomson aside and told him, "Bobby, if you ever hit one, hit one now." Talk about pressure!

With fans at the Polo Grounds on their feet and people across the country watching and waiting, Thomson stepped into the batter's box and tried to concentrate.

The first pitch came in—a fastball down the middle. Thomson didn't swing, and it was called for strike one. The second pitch was another fastball, and this time Thomson didn't hesitate. He smoked a sharp line drive headed straight for the 315-foot mark painted on the left field fence. The Dodgers' left fielder thought it might bounce off the wall and got ready to field the ball.

But you already know how this story ends. The ball never touched that wall. It sailed over the fence and into the stands for a home run to win the game, 5-4. The stunned Dodgers walked slowly off the field as Bobby Thomson joyfully bounced his way around the bases, finally jumping into a crowd of Giants players and coaches who had swarmed around home plate.

The Giants had done the impossible. They'd come all the way back from 13½ games out to beat the Dodgers and win the National League pennant. The radio announcer for the Giants, Russ Hodges, was so excited that he just shouted over and over, "THE GIANTS WIN THE PENNANT! THE GIANTS WIN THE PENNANT! THE GIANTS WIN THE PENNANT!"

The next day, the New York newspapers proclaimed Thomson's homer "The Shot Heard 'Round the World." Now that might be a bit of an exaggeration—newspaper headlines can be like that sometimes. But in fact there were lots of young U.S. soldiers who took a break from the Korean War to follow the exciting pennant race and listen to the game broadcast on Armed Forces Radio. So Thomson's shot really was heard 'round the world.

Now, more than a half-century later, most people don't even remember (or care) that the Giants went on to lose the 1951 World Series to the Yankees. But they'll never forget Bobby Thomson and his legendary home run.

WILLIE MAYS: THE FIVE-TOOL PLAYER

WILLIE MAYS ONCE SAID, "I think I was the best baseball player I ever saw." That may sound like bragging, but it's really just the honest truth. And he's not the only one with that opinion.

Fans lucky enough to watch him play during his 22 years with the Giants knew they were seeing a truly special ballplayer, a uniquely talented athlete whose skill was matched only by his love for the game. His cheerful greeting led to the nickname "The Say Hey Kid," but many people just knew him simply as "Willie," as in, "Did you see that incredible play Willie made today?"

So what was it about Willie Mays that made him so special?

The answer can be found in the tools he brought to the ballpark every day.

Different baseball players have different strengths and abilities. Some players are dependable hitters, while others are big sluggers. Some might be speedy baserunners. Some have strong throwing arms, and others are known as rangy and reliable fielders. The best major league players typically combine three or even four of these skills, but it is rare to find a "five-tool player" who excels at them all. Willie Mays was the classic five-tool player.

Tool #1: Hitting for average

Willie Mays was an excellent hitter even before he got to the major leagues. When he was first signed by the Giants, he played for their minor-league team in New Jersey and batted .353. Then he was brought up to the AAA team in Minneapolis, the last stop before the majors. He played about a month there and batted an astounding .477.

That was enough to catch the attention of the Giants' manager, Leo Durocher, who called up Mays in the middle of the 1951 season. Willie was only 20 years old, but "The Say Hey Kid" had a huge impact on the Giants. He contributed several key hits as his team fought from 13½ games back to force the famous playoff series with the Dodgers. Mays was named Rookie of the Year, and his career was off to an impressive start.

But just 34 games into his second major league season in 1952, Willie Mays was drafted by the U.S. Army. He had to leave the Giants and serve in the military for two years. When he finally returned to the ballclub, Willie didn't have too much trouble getting readjusted. In fact, he led the league in hitting that year, batting .345 with 195 hits and 41 home runs on his way to an MVP award. Not bad for someone coming back from two years off!

Mays didn't stop getting hits until he'd collected 3,283 of them. He batted over .300 ten times in his career and finished with a lifetime average of .302. Said Willie simply, "They throw the ball, I hit it."

Tool #2: Hitting for power

After his first few games in the majors, Willie Mays was worried. He hadn't gotten a single hit in his first 12 at bats, and he thought maybe he wasn't ready for the big leagues after all. But Durocher reassured the youngster, promising Mays that he would be the starting center fielder for as long as Leo was manager.

When the Giants returned from their road trip for a game against Boston, more than 23,000 curious New York fans headed to the Polo Grounds to check out the team's new centerfielder for the first time.

In the first inning, with two outs, Mays came up to bat against Boston's ace left-hander, the great Warren Spahn. Willie finally broke out of his slump with a monstrous home run that not only cleared the fence— it sailed up and over the roof of the stadium! Years later, Spahn recalled that home run and said he'd never forgive himself for not pitching more carefully to the struggling rookie. He said, with a smile, "We might have gotten rid of Willie forever if I'd only struck him out."

This dramatic first home run was just the beginning for Mays, who went on to hit 20 round-trippers in his rookie season. When he returned to the team in 1954 after his military stint, he hit 41 homers, and he followed that up with a league-leading 51 the next season.

Willie also had a way of getting the big hit when his team needed it most. He still holds the Major League record for home runs hit in extra innings (22).

Over his 22-year career, Willie Mays hit a total of 660 home runs, which placed him third on the all-time list behind only Babe Ruth and Hank Aaron—until his godson, Barry Bonds, surpassed them all. Some people think that if Mays had gotten to play in those two seasons he spent in the Army, he might have had a chance at breaking Ruth's record himself.

Tool #3: Running

Willie Mays was fast. His mother had been a track star in high school, so perhaps he inherited his unusual speed from her. Wherever it came from, it was clearly a gift, and one that helped him in every aspect of the game, including hitting, fielding, and baserunning.

Mays was not just fast, though. He was also a very smart baserunner. While he was running, he would always think about where the defense was playing and who else was on the basepaths so he could judge his own chances of advancing safely.

Although he led the league in stolen bases from 1956 through 1959, his great speed could not be fully appreciated with that statistic alone. He also found creative ways to score from second on a bunt, or to motor from first to third on a wild pitch.

His speed and daring on the bases drove opposing pitchers crazy, but it made Willie Mays an especially exciting player to watch. As he streaked around the bases, he'd be flying so fast that his cap would come off as he rounded second and headed to third. His teammates later revealed that Willie purposely wore his hats either one size too small or too big to make sure that happened!

Tool #4: Throwing

Most people know that Willie Mays was a great fielder, but not everyone remembers that he also had a very strong and accurate throwing arm. In fact, baseball legend Joe DiMaggio once said that Mays had the best throwing arm in baseball.

Though Mays made countless great throws, one particularly memorable play happened during his rookie season on August 15, 1951. The Giants had won four straight and were just a few games into their historic comeback. They were playing against the rival Dodgers, who at that point still had a very comfortable 11½ game lead.

The score was tied, 1-1, in the top of the eighth inning. The Dodgers had Billy Cox, one of their fastest runners, in scoring position at third base. With one out, Carl Furillo came up to bat and launched a long fly ball to deep center field, at least 400 feet from home plate. Even if Mays caught the ball, it looked like Cox would easily tag up and score the go-ahead run.

Mays did make the catch, reaching up with his glove

as he ran full-speed toward the ball, just as Cox tagged up at third. Willie knew there was no time to stop, turn around, and make the throw home. So he just let the momentum of the ball hitting his glove spin him completely around. Whirling like a discus thrower, he fired the ball to catcher Wes Westrum, who put the tag on a very surprised Cox sliding desperately into home plate. The crowd at first was silent, not sure whether to believe what they'd just seen. Then the umpire called Cox out, and the fans burst into applause.

Even the Dodgers' manager, Charlie Dressen, couldn't believe Willie had really made that play. After the Giants ended up winning, 3-1, Dressen said grudgingly, "Well, that's a good play. But I'd like to see him do it again."

Tool #5: Fielding

For all his accomplishments in hitting, running, and throwing, Willie Mays is probably best remembered for his spectacular defensive play in center field.

Throughout his major league career, Mays found a way to make seemingly impossible catches look routine. He always said that "If the ball went up, I could catch it." One time he even smashed into the center field wall so hard that he knocked himself unconscious—but he still held on to the ball!

His teammates learned to watch for Willie to thump his glove, which was a sign that he was sure to catch a ball heading toward him. He was also famous for his signature "basket catches," which he made holding his glove face-up at waist level, like a basket.

New York's Polo Grounds, where Mays started his career, had very short fences in left and right field but a notoriously deep center field (483 feet!). So there was plenty of territory for the young, speedy Mays to cover. He made many memorable catches there, but none more famous than one play known simply as "The Catch."

It was Game 1 of the 1954 World Series. The Giants were playing the Cleveland Indians, and the score was tied 2-2 in the top of the eighth inning. New York's starting pitcher, Sal Maglie, had walked two batters, and Durocher brought in a reliever to face the Indians' left-handed slugger Vic Wertz. On the fourth pitch, Wertz crushed a long fly ball to deep center field. Mays, who had been playing relatively shallow, immediately turned his back to home plate and started running.

Wertz's ball was hit so deep that there didn't seem to be any chance of Mays catching it. In any other ball-park, it would certainly have been a home run.

But Mays kept running, watching the ball over his shoulder like a wide receiver in football. As he ran, he thumped his glove, and then, to the amazement of everyone, he pulled in the impossible catch nearly 450 feet from home plate!

But he wasn't done yet. Mays immediately turned and threw, whirling around so fast that he fell over (and yes, his cap fell off too). He hit the cutoff man at second base and kept the runners from scoring. The Giants escaped from the jam, won the game in the tenth inning, and went on to sweep the World Series.

Almost everyone who watched the game that day declared Willie's catch the most amazing play they'd ever seen. Mays himself said simply, "I had it all the way."

The first Gold Glove awards for outstanding defensive play were handed out in 1957. Of course, Willie won that year—and for the next twelve straight years as well! No outfielder has won more.

"The other magic ingredient"

But there was even more to Willie Mays than those five baseball "tools." To this day, he is remembered for more than just his great skill at all phases of the game. When people talk about Mays, they use words like "enthusiasm" and "exuberance" to try and express the energy and joy that Willie Mays brought to the game. He loved playing baseball and never understood why other players said it was such hard work. Though he played until he was 42 years old, he always seemed to be having as much fun as a little kid. In fact, even as a big-leaguer, Willie used to go out and play stickball on the streets of Harlem with his young fans.

His first Giants manager, Leo Durocher, knew from the start that Willie Mays would be great. Durocher described Mays like this: "He could do the five things you have to do to be a superstar: hit, hit with power, run, throw, and field. And he had the other magic ingredient that turns a superstar into a super Superstar. Charisma. He lit the room up when he came in. He was a joy to be around."

And that, in the end, is what truly made Willie Mays one of the all-time greatest players in baseball.

GOING, GOING, GONE

IMAGINE: YOU'RE A YOUNG KID in 1957. You've grown up in New York City, so of course you're a baseball fan. You root for the Giants because you live in upper Manhattan and your dad was a Giants fan (just like his dad before him). When you go to the Polo Grounds to watch a game, he tells you stories about the great players he remembers—legendary names like Hubbell and Terry and Ott. He likes to remind his buddies from Brooklyn that the Giants have won 14 National League pennants. Those Dodger "bums" have only 9.

Your whole family cheered wildly when Bobby Thomson hit the home run in '51 to beat the Dodgers. You remember watching on TV when Willie Mays robbed Vic Wertz and the Giants went on to sweep the Indians in the '54 Series. You and your pals like to try to imitate that famous basket catch, and you always get to the ballpark early so you can watch Willie and your other favorite players take batting practice.

Sure, the team hasn't been doing so great the last couple of seasons, finishing as far back as sixth place. But you still love your Giants.

Then, one day, you read in the paper that the team is moving. Leaving New York. Going way out west to California. San Francisco, for crying out loud. It might as well be the moon.

How could this have happened?

Unfortunately for young fans everywhere, major league baseball is (and always has been) a business. And for Horace Stoneham, the owner of the Giants since 1936, it simply didn't make good business sense to keep the Giants in New York any longer.

New York had a huge population of dedicated baseball fans. But the city also had three major league teams—the Giants, Dodgers, and Yankees—and the Giants had never drawn as many fans as the other two. Their historic but outdated ballpark, the Polo Grounds, was going to be demolished to make room for a new housing development. So Stoneham needed to find his team a new home somewhere. He thought Minnesota might be good, since the Giants already had their AAA team and a decent ballpark there.

Meanwhile, across town, Dodgers owner Walter O'Malley was facing a similar dilemma. He wanted to build his own ballpark to replace Ebbets Field but couldn't find a suitable site in Brooklyn. After purchasing a minor league franchise in southern California, O'Malley began quietly meeting with officials there to discuss possibly moving his team to Los Angeles.

As you know, the Giants and Dodgers have always had an intense rivalry on the field, and that competition was very good for both owners. Even when the teams weren't doing well, fans would always pay to come out and see the Giants and Dodgers battle. So from a business point of view, it didn't make any sense to split up the rivalry by moving one team to California and one to Minnesota.

O'Malley suggested that Stoneham take a look at San Francisco instead. He'd heard that their new mayor, George Christopher, really wanted to bring major league baseball to his city.

At the time, San Francisco had a very successful minor-league team called the Seals. In 1957, the Seals were in first place in their Pacific Coast League and regularly drawing more fans to their tiny little ballpark than the mighty New York Giants could get to come out to the Polo Grounds. And many great major league stars, including Joe DiMaggio, had their roots in the San Francisco Bay Area.

Secretly, Mayor Christopher began flying to New York to meet with Stoneham and O'Malley. He didn't want to attract any attention from reporters, so he stayed in seedy hotels in the not-so-nice parts of town so nobody would even know he was there.

Together they put together a plan to have both teams move west together. At that time, it seemed like a crazy proposition. There were no major league teams west of St. Louis, let alone as far away as California, so this move would mean a huge change for all of baseball. Rumors started swirling, but nobody believed these two great teams would really leave New York.

By August of 1957, Stoneham had made up his mind. When he announced that the Giants would move to San Francisco, he angered and disappointed thousands of loyal fans. Though he knew it was the best business decision, it was still hard to uproot a team with so much history and tradition in New York. "I feel bad about the kids," Stoneham told reporters, "but I haven't seen many of their fathers lately."

A few months later, O'Malley confirmed that his

team would also move to Los Angeles, breaking even more hearts in Brooklyn.

And so, in 1958, both teams packed up their bats, their balls, and their bitter rivalry, and headed west for the start of a brand new era in baseball.

NEW HOMETOWN HEROES

IT ALMOST NEVER SNOWS in San Francisco. But on April 14, 1958, a blizzard fell on Montgomery Street.

This was no ordinary snowstorm, but a glittering shower of confetti that swirled down from the skyscrapers and piled in drifts below as the city hosted a grand ticker-tape parade to welcome its newest residents: the San Francisco Giants. Major league baseball had finally come to California, and thousands of fans crowded the city streets to greet their new hometown heroes.

Huge banners and homemade signs proclaimed "WELCOME S.F. GIANTS" in different languages. Downtown streets were filled with cheering crowds of curious city dwellers, lucky kids who got to sneak out of school, and businessmen wearing suits and hats. The festive parade included marching bands, Scottish bagpipers, Chinese dancers, and cheerleaders. The Giants players themselves rode in open convertibles, waving to their enthusiastic new fans and occasionally stopping to bat away colorful balloons bouncing through the air.

It was quite a welcome party, to be sure. And the fun continued the next day, when more than 23,000 fans packed into cozy little Seals Stadium to see the Giants take on their arch-rival Dodgers in the first major league baseball game ever played on the west coast.

Fans and players loved the "intimate" (a nice way of saying "small") Seals Stadium, which had previously been the home for two Pacific Coast League teams, the Missions and the Seals. It was a completely open-air stadium with just a single level of seats, so the fans were close to the players and the action on the field. With a fresh coat of dark green paint and other improvements for the major league team, Seals Stadium would be the Giants' ballpark for their first two years in San Francisco.

As they took the field at the start of the 1958 season, the Giants had only a few stars left from their days in New York. Willie Mays was still there, of course, but the team also had quite a few new faces and unproven rookies. During those seasons at Seals, however, two

43

young players quickly emerged as the first "home-grown" San Francisco stars: Orlando Cepeda and Willie McCovey.

Orlando Cepeda grew up in Puerto Rico and was among the first Latin American players to break into the major leagues. His father, Pedro Cepeda, had been a great baseball player, widely known as the Babe Ruth of Latin America. Pedro's nickname was "Perucho" or "The Bull," so his son Orlando soon became known as "Baby Bull."

Orlando was a very talented young player, and he was signed by scouts from the Giants at the age of 17. After spending a few years in America trying to prove he could play big-league baseball, Orlando Cepeda finally got his chance in 1958.

Upon his arrival at spring training, he quickly impressed his Giants coaches and teammates. Manager Bill Rigney asked veteran Whitey Lockman what he thought about Cepeda.

"He's a year away," replied Lockman.

A year away from what? The major leagues?

"The Hall of Fame."

Once the season started, the "Baby Bull" wasted no time in making believers of the Giants fans as well. On that Opening Day in 1958, when he first came to the plate wearing jersey number 30, most people had never even heard of the kid with the exotic-sounding name.

But then, in the fifth inning, in only his second major league at bat, Cepeda blasted one out of the park for a home run, the first major league homer ever hit on the west coast. The Giants soundly thrashed the hated Dodgers, 8-0, and San Francisco fans had a brand new hero they could embrace as one of their very own.

Cepeda went on to have a fantastic year in 1958. He batted .312, hit 25 homers, knocked in 96 runs, and led the National League with 38 doubles. He was unanimously chosen as the NL Rookie of the Year.

Willie Mays, who had been a Rookie of the Year himself back in 1951, spoke with admiration of his young teammate: "He is annoying every pitcher in the league. He is strong, he hits to all fields, and he makes all the plays. He's the most relaxed first-year man I ever saw."

The next year was 1959. About halfway through the season, the Giants introduced another new prospect: a young left-handed slugger named Willie McCovey. He wore number 44 in honor of his idol, Hank Aaron, who was from the same hometown of Mobile, Alabama.

McCovey was called up in the middle of the season after swatting 29 homers in the minors, and like Cepeda, he immediately got off to a great start. McCovey went 4-for-4 in his major league debut on July 30, hitting two singles and two triples off future Hall of Famer Robin Roberts. Suddenly the San Francisco fans found themselves cheering for another new hero.

"Stretch" McCovey finished his rookie year with a .354 batting average and 13 home runs in only 52 games. Despite playing less than half a season, McCovey won the National League Rookie of the Year award by a unanimous vote—just like Cepeda the year before.

A towering presence at the plate, the 6'4" McCovey was called "the scariest hitter in baseball" by Bob Gibson. That's quite a compliment, coming from one of the game's scariest pitchers!

In time, pitchers learned to walk "Big Mac" rather than throw him a fat pitch that might end up in the bleachers. They didn't have much choice, because as famed manager Sparky Anderson once said, "If you pitch to him, he'll ruin baseball. He'd hit 80 home runs."

Well, Willie McCovey never quite hit 80 home runs in a season, but he did launch a total of 521 homers during his historic career. He was also known as a true gentleman, both on and off the field. In his honor, the Giants present the "Willie Mac" award each year to a player who demonstrates the kind of team spirit and leadership that made McCovey a legend in San Francisco.

And "Baby Bull" Orlando Cepeda, despite battling chronic knee problems for much of his career, hit 379 career homers of his own and batted .297 over 17 seasons in the majors. Though he was traded to the Cardinals in 1966, he remains one of the most beloved Giants of all time.

Both Cepeda and McCovey would eventually be inducted into the Baseball Hall of Fame and have their numbers retired by the San Francisco Giants.

Of course, the fans sitting in the bleachers at Seals Stadium in 1959 didn't know any of that yet. They just knew these kids were fun to watch.

In just two short years, Cepeda, McCovey, Mays and the rest of the Giants had won the hearts of San Francisco. As the honeymoon in Seals Stadium drew to a close and the team prepared to move into a shiny new ballpark, fans couldn't wait to see what their hometown heroes would do next.

LIFE AT THE 'STICK

PARKING SPACES. THAT'S ALL he really cared about—lots and lots of parking spaces. Ten thousand, to be exact.

When Giants owner Horace Stoneham agreed to move his team to San Francisco, he insisted that the city build an all-new stadium with at least 10,000 parking spaces. Stoneham felt that limited parking at the Polo Grounds in New York had kept fans away, and he didn't want to make the same mistake again.

Players and fans loved cozy little Seals Stadium, where the Giants played during their first two seasons in San Francisco. But it could only seat about 23,000 fans and was simply too small to be the permanent home for a major league team. Adding a second deck for more seats was a popular idea at the time, but there was still no room for the 10,000 parking spaces Stoneham wanted. So the team could not stay at Seals Stadium.

Some city leaders proposed building a downtown ballpark, but Stoneham rejected that idea because—you guessed it—there wouldn't be enough parking.

There was one spot, however, that had plenty of space for parking at a price the city could afford: a strip of land sticking out into San Francisco Bay called Candlestick Point.

An architect drew up plans for a brand new state-of-the-art stadium, and construction began during the summer of 1958. Two years later, at the start of the 1960 season, Candlestick Park was ready for the Giants to move in.

This was the first new stadium built in America in over twenty years, and its unique concrete-and-steel design was like a space-age vision of the future. When Vice President Richard Nixon threw out the first pitch before 42,269 fans on Opening Day in 1960, he was so impressed that he declared Candlestick Park "the finest ballpark in America."

That did not turn out to be the case.

Fans at Candlestick had some gorgeous views, especially since the outfield was left open to the bay. Unfortunately, this also meant that the entire ballpark was exposed to the freezing winds that blew in every afternoon across the bay.

The architects had designed some special features to deal with the wind. They built the stadium close to a hill, which they figured would provide some protection. They designed a special boomerang-shaped baffle around the top of the stadium, which was expected to block out the wind. They even installed hot water pipes below the seats, which were supposed to help raise the temperature as much as 20 degrees on chilly San Francisco nights.

Unfortunately, none of these "solutions" could tame the beastly weather at Candlestick. The fierce winds continued to blow. In fact, scientists now know that the hill and the special baffle might have actually made things worse. And the fancy built-in heating system was a complete failure.

It's true that a day game at Candlestick Park could be downright pleasant in the warm California sunshine. But almost every afternoon, the damp fog rolled in and the frigid winds started to howl. Fans going to night games soon learned they had to bundle up for an Arctic expedition: heavy jackets, wool blankets, scarves, gloves, hats—even earmuffs!

Players, meanwhile, had to adjust to the severe

conditions down on the field. The icy wind that was freezing the fans also blew fly balls off course and knocked the caps right off players' heads. The wind whipped so unpredictably that, according to shortstop Ed Broussoud, "Your pants could be blowing in while your shirt was blowing out."

Hot dog wrappers and soda cups blew around the field in swirling dust clouds, littering the diamond with debris. After his very first game at the 'Stick, Willie McCovey complained, "Peanut shells kept getting in my eyes."

Outfielders were often fooled by seemingly routine pop flies that were suddenly seized by the wind. Out in center field, Willie Mays no longer started running as soon as a fly ball was hit. Instead, he learned to freeze and silently count "1…2…3…4…5…" while he waited to see which way the tricky winds would blow the ball.

The wind also affected batters at Candlestick, especially right-handed hitters like Mays and Cepeda. The strong jetstream that blew in from left field knocked down hard-hit balls that might have sailed over the fence in other parks, turning potential home runs into harmless pop-ups.

Candlestick Park soon became infamous for these miserable playing conditions. In 1961, San Francisco hosted the All-Star Game, and the Giants' own Stu Miller was pitching in relief in the top of the ninth inning. As he took the mound, the trademark Candlestick winds were whipping through the ballpark. The flags in the outfield flapped so hard they looked like they might fly right off the poles.

The National League was winning 3-2, but the American League had two men on base. As Miller looked for the sign from his catcher, an especially big gust of wind blew toward the mound, and he wavered a bit trying to keep his balance. At first, the umpire didn't know what to do. After the American League players complained, he reluctantly called a balk. "What can I do?" he asked Miller. "Rules are rules."

The headlines in newspapers around the country the next day declared: "STU MILLER BLOWN OFF MOUND." Though the accounts were clearly exaggerated, the legend persists to this day.

Another favorite Candlestick story comes from 1963, when the New York Mets were taking batting practice and watched the wind pick up the entire batting cage—and drop it at the pitcher's mound 60 feet away!

In 1971, seats were added to the outfield to enclose the stadium, which everyone hoped would cut down on the wind. But this plan backfired. The gusts just swirled more powerfully and unpredictably than ever.

Years later, when a reporter asked Giants slugger Jack Clark what would improve Candlestick Park, he had a one-word response: "Dynamite."

In the 1980s, the Giants decided to offer a special badge of honor called the "Croix de Candlestick." It was presented to those loyal fans who endured the miserable conditions and stayed until the end of extra-inning night games. The pin featured the "SF" logo covered in ice, with the Latin inscription "VENI · VIDI · VIXI," which means "I came. I saw. I survived."

In the end, the Giants and their fans did survive. Candlestick Park was their home for forty years, and some of the greatest stories in team history unfolded there. It was the park everyone loved to hate, but many longtime Giants fans have warm memories even for the freezing cold 'Stick.

And at least there was always plenty of parking!

1962: THE BEST EVER?

WHICH SAN FRANCISCO GIANTS team was the best? For many long-time fans, the answer is easy.

The 1962 Giants had Willie Mays, Willie McCovey, and Orlando Cepeda terrorizing opposing pitchers. They had a superb starting rotation with veteran pitchers Billy Pierce, Jack Sanford, and Billy O'Dell joined by a young Juan Marichal. And in the late innings, they could count on reliever Stu Miller to put out any fires. With key contributions from these stars and other great players like Felipe Alou and Jim Davenport, the club won an incredible 103 games that year.

Down in Los Angeles, meanwhile, the Dodgers had assembled an impressive roster of their own. Their offensive star was speedy shortstop Maury Wills, who was named the league MVP after stealing 104 bases, breaking a record set by Ty Cobb way back in 1915. The Dodgers' pitching staff also featured two all-time greats: Don Drysdale, who led the league that year with 25 wins, and Sandy Koufax, who had the lowest ERA at 2.54.

Just five years after they'd arrived in sunny California, these two teams had reignited the intense Giants-Dodgers rivalry. West coast fans were captivated as the teams battled throughout the season in another thrilling pennant race.

The Giants started out hot and held first place until early June, when the Dodgers took over the lead. The teams leapfrogged each other in the standings over the next two months, but by early August, the Dodgers had built a 5½ game lead over the Giants. As the L.A. team headed into a three-game series at Candlestick Park, the Giants knew they had to win to stay alive.

Giants manager Alvin Dark came up with a unique way to slow down Wills, the Dodgers' pesky base-stealer. Dark told his groundskeepers to water the area around first base more than usual, making it too soft and muddy for Wills to get a good jump off first.

As you might expect, the Dodgers complained, so the umpires ordered the Giants to add more dirt to the area. But that just made the ground even more unstable, like quicksand. It was so bad that Dodgers first baseman Ron Fairly began building sand castles in protest.

Dark's sneaky strategy seemed to work, though. With their swift runners slowed by the soggy speed trap at first base, the Dodgers lost all three games, and the Giants were back in the race. For the rest of his career, Alvin Dark would be known to Dodgers fans as "The Swamp Fox."

The Giants continued to nip at the Dodgers' heels as summer turned into fall. On the last day of the regular season, Los Angeles had a one-game lead, and the Giants were down to their last gasp. But a home run by Willie Mays in the eighth inning helped San Francisco beat Houston, 2-1. The Dodgers could have clinched the pennant with a win, but they ended up losing at home, 1-0, to the St. Louis Cardinals.

That left both teams tied with 101 regular-season wins apiece. They'd have to play a three-game playoff to decide who would go to the World Series.

This whole scenario seemed very familiar to baseball fans everywhere. Only eleven years earlier, the New York Giants had come from behind to tie the hated Brooklyn Dodgers on the last day of the season and force a three-game playoff. That series ended triumphantly for the Giants with Bobby Thomson's "Shot

Heard 'Round the World."

Could the Giants do it again?

It certainly looked like they could in Game 1 of the 1962 playoff series. San Francisco pitcher Billy Pierce allowed only three hits, Willie Mays hit two home runs, and the Giants won easily, 8-0.

In Game 2, San Francisco jumped out to a 5-0 lead, but L.A. scored seven runs in the bottom of the sixth. The Dodgers went on to win, 8-7, in a game that lasted more than four hours.

The calendar said 1962, but it felt like 1951 all over again as the entire season came down to a deciding Game 3. Once again, the survivor would earn the National League pennant and the right to face the Yankees in the World Series.

In front of more than 40,000 L.A. fans at Dodger Stadium, the Giants went ahead 2-0 in the third inning. But the Dodgers came back to take the lead in the sixth, and then in the seventh Maury Wills stole two bases and scored on an error, putting the Dodgers ahead 4-2. The Giants went into the ninth inning down two runs and needing a miracle like the one they'd gotten in the Polo Grounds years before.

There would be no dramatic home run this time, though. Instead, Matty Alou started things off with a single. After a groundout, McCovey walked. Then Felipe Alou walked. Suddenly the bases were filled with Giants, and Willie Mays was stepping into the batter's box.

On the very first pitch he saw, "The Say Hey Kid" lined a single up the middle, scoring one run. In came L.A. reliever Stan Williams, hoping to snuff out the comeback. But Cepeda greeted him with a sacrifice fly, and the score was tied.

It didn't stop there, because the Dodgers seemed to be collapsing. Wild pitch. Walk. Another walk, and a run scored. Error, and another run.

By the time they were done, the scrappy Giants had scored four runs in the top of the ninth to take the lead, 6-4. Ace pitcher Billy Pierce held on for the save to give the Giants the win and unleash a huge city-wide party back home. The San Francisco Giants had won their first pennant!

The players couldn't spend too much time celebrating, though—they had to get back to Candlestick Park the very next day to play the New York Yankees in Game 1 of the World Series.

Not surprisingly, the ballclub was exhausted from the tight playoff games against the Dodgers, and they lost Game 1 to the Yankees. But the Giants quickly recovered to win Game 2 and even the series.

Then the teams flew back to New York for three games and again traded victories, with the Yankees taking Game 3, the Giants winning Game 4, and the Yankees prevailing in Game 5 to give them a 3-2 lead in the Series. The Yankees and Giants would have to come back to San Francisco to decide the World Series. The devoted fans in the city by the bay couldn't wait.

Unfortunately, they would have to. The Giants hadn't had a single game rained out in 1962, but Typhoon Freda hit San Francisco that week and postponed Game 6 for three days. Both teams had to go into the drier Central Valley just to practice, and the delay was frustrating to the players, coaches and fans.

The heavy rains made the field conditions at Candlestick so bad that the team called in helicopters to hover just above the turf in an effort to blow the ground dry. It didn't seem to help.

Finally, on October 15, the teams met on a soggy field in Game 6. For the Giants, it was worth the wait. A well-rested Billy Pierce shut down the Bronx Bombers on only three hits, and the Giants knocked the great Whitey Ford out of the game in the fifth inning on their way to a 5-2 victory.

Once again, the never-say-die Giants had fought

back from the brink. They were one win away from the World Series championship.

Game 7 was a classic pitchers' duel, with the Yankees' Ralph Terry matching up against the Giants' Jack Sanford for the third time in the Series. The New Yorkers managed to scrape together one run in the fifth inning and were still leading, 1-0, going into the bottom of the ninth.

The San Francisco fans held their breath, hoping and praying for just one more miracle.

Matty Alou got things started in the ninth with a perfect drag bunt single. Terry quickly responded, though, by striking out Matty's brother Felipe and the next batter, Chuck Hiller.

The Giants were down to their final out. But they had Willie Mays coming up to bat, and he loved being at the plate in critical situations like this one. Willie knew he could win the game and the World Series with one swing of the bat.

"I was thinking home run," he said.

Mays took two balls and then swung and missed at Terry's third offering for a strike. On the next pitch, Mays sliced a drive toward the right field corner, a certain extra-base hit. Alou was running on contact and tore around second base.

The outfield was still soaked from all the rain, and the wet grass slowed the ball down. Right fielder Roger Maris got to it quickly and threw to the cutoff man, holding Mays to a double. Alou, meanwhile, raced around to third but was held there by the third-base coach.

What would have happened if Alou had tried to score? Giants fans will always wonder.

The game wasn't over yet. The Giants had the tying run on third, the winning run on second, and the imposing Willie McCovey looming in the on-deck circle.

The Yankees manager walked to the mound and asked Terry if he wanted to pitch to McCovey (who had hit a home run off him in Game 2) or walk him intentionally and face Orlando Cepeda instead. Terry chose to pitch to "Big Mac."

McCovey swung at the first pitch and drove it high and deep—but the fierce Candlestick winds pushed it foul. The fans groaned.

When Terry followed up with an inside fastball, McCovey was ready. With one loud crack of the bat, he smashed a low line drive into short right center.

"It was the hardest ball I ever hit," said McCovey later.

But, to the dismay of McCovey and the stunned Giants fans, his blazing shot was just within reach of Yankees second baseman Bobby Richardson. In a mere fraction of a second, Richardson stuck out his glove and speared the ball for the final out, clinching the World Series victory for the Yankees.

This time, by just an inch or two, the Giants had run out of miracles. The stinging heartbreak still lingers for McCovey and all the fans who remember that thrilling '62 season. They couldn't know it at the time, but it would be their last, best shot at a World Series crown for many years.

MARICHAL VS. SPAHN

THE VERY FIRST TIME Juan Marichal took the mound for the San Francisco Giants, he nearly pitched a no-hitter.

It was July 19, 1960, and fans and teammates watched in amazement as the young pitcher from the Dominican Republic mowed down one Philadelphia batter after another. Finally, with two outs in the eighth inning, the Phillies broke the drought with a single, but that was all the Philadelphia offense could muster. Marichal struck out twelve and walked only one as the Giants won 2-0, and the "Dominican Dandy" became an instant fan favorite.

With his extremely high leg-kick and remarkable control of a wide variety of pitches, Marichal would go on to win 243 games in his career. He posted an incredible lifetime ERA of 2.89 on his way to Cooperstown, and his number 27 was retired by the Giants.

But for all the wonderful memories he gave Giants fans over his 14 years with the team, there is one game that stands out more than any other. On July 2, 1963, Marichal started a night game at Candlestick Park that turned out to be one of the most dramatic pitching battles of all time.

On the hill for the Milwaukee Braves that evening was Warren Spahn, who at 42 years old was winding down his Hall of Fame career but was still a dominating pitcher. Earlier in the season Spahn had broken the record for most career wins by a left-hander. He came into the game with an 11-3 record and had won his last five games in a row—not bad for an "old man."

Marichal was only 25 years old but was having his best season yet. He was on an eight-game winning streak with a record of 12-3. Just two weeks earlier, he had become the first Giant to throw a no-hitter since Carl Hubbell back in 1929.

Though it was a chilly night game at Candlestick, more than 15,000 fans showed up expecting to see a great pitching duel. They got even more than they bargained for.

Through the first three innings, each team could

manage just one hit. But then the Braves' superstar slugger, Hank Aaron, hammered a Marichal offering to left field to lead off the fourth. As the fans craned their necks and Aaron settled into his home run trot, the famous Candlestick winds knocked the ball down and into the waiting glove of Willie McCovey. Hank trotted back to the dugout, and the game was still scoreless.

The fifth inning came and went, and so did the sixth. The score remained 0-0.

In the top of the seventh, as Marichal worked through the Braves' lineup for the third time, Spahn stepped to the plate and tried to take matters into his own hands. He swung at a high curveball and lined it off the very top of the right field fence for a long double. But he advanced no farther as the Dominican Dandy got the next batter to ground out harmlessly to first.

Inning after inning, Marichal and Spahn kept both teams off the scoreboard. A few batters managed to get on base, but that only made the pitchers bear down even harder, and nobody crossed the plate.

As Spahn walked out to the mound to start the bottom of the ninth inning, the score was still tied 0-0. He knew he would be facing the heart of the Giants' lineup: Mays, McCovey, Alou, and Cepeda. The San

Francisco fans hoped that one of these All-Stars could win the game with a single swing.

Willie Mays grounded out to start the inning. Then it was Willie McCovey's turn. With a powerful swing, he launched one deep to right field. The ball kept rising and rising. The San Francisco crowd erupted in celebration as the ball sailed up and out of the stadium.

But then the umpire waved it foul!

With the fans still buzzing in protest, McCovey was retired on a grounder. Felipe Alou kept the Giants' hopes alive with a single, but Spahn got Orlando Cepeda to hit a pop-up for the third out. After nine regulation innings, the scoreboard was goose-eggs all the way across.

At this point Marichal and Spahn had each thrown what would normally be a complete-game shutout. But of course the game wasn't yet complete. And neither pitcher was ready to give in.

So they kept playing. The tenth inning went by, and then the eleventh, twelfth, and thirteenth. Still there was no score. And still Marichal and Spahn stayed in the game.

Marichal had retired 16 batters in a row and actually seemed to be getting stronger. On the other side, Spahn continued to baffle the Giants. The remaining fans at

Candlestick huddled together for warmth but knew they were seeing a game for the ages.

Between innings, both managers checked with their pitchers. The stubborn Spahn still wouldn't yield to the bullpen. Marichal was tired but told Alvin Dark, "Do you see that man on the mound? That man is 42 and I'm 25. I'm not ready for you to take me out."

So they kept playing. Incredibly, the game was still scoreless after fifteen innings. Marichal pitched the top of inning number sixteen but feared that would have to be his last. He had already thrown 227 pitches.

After he got the third out, he waited on the mound for the rest of the team to run in. As they walked back to the dugout, Marichal quietly told Mays that he thought he was done.

"Don't worry," said Mays. "I'm going to win this game for you."

Willie kept his word. At well past midnight, with one out in the bottom of the sixteenth inning, Spahn threw another of his classic screwballs. This one stayed over the middle of the plate, and Mays sent it deep into the night for a solo home run to finally win the game, 1-0.

"Man, I was tired," said Willie afterwards. "I just wanted to go home."

SPITBALLS AND A MOON SHOT

TO THROW A SPITBALL, a pitcher takes some spit (or mud or grease or hair tonic or anything else he can get his hands on) and secretly rubs it on one side of the ball to make the pitch dip and dart unpredictably as it crosses the plate.

Technically, the spitball was outlawed in 1920. In the late 1960s, the rules became stricter. Pitchers weren't even allowed to put their hands to their mouth while on the mound. But many pitchers continued to throw the "spitter" anyway; they just had to be sneakier about it. And nobody did it better than Gaylord Perry.

Perry was a right-handed Hall of Fame hurler who wore number 36 for the Giants from 1962 to 1971 and is best remembered for his notorious trademark pitch.

Perry didn't always throw the spitball. He didn't

have to. He kept hitters off-balance because they never knew when it was coming. He loved to play an elaborate game of cat-and-mouse with his opponents, often going through odd rituals on the mound that were designed to make them think he was throwing a spitter, even when he wasn't.

Everyone assumed that Perry must have been hiding some slippery substance that he was rubbing on the ball. He teased batters by playing right along with these suspicions. He'd rub his neck, tug at his shirt, touch his hat, adjust his belt, and smooth his pants—often with a sly grin on his face. These antics rattled umpires and infuriated opposing managers, many of whom tried countless times to catch Perry in the act of doctoring the ball.

Once, a first-base umpire crept up behind Perry and knocked off his cap to see if he had hidden something there. Another time, manager Billy Martin threatened to bring in bloodhounds to sniff the baseballs. Sometimes umpires would force Perry to go back to the clubhouse and change his jersey or his pants if they thought he was hiding something they couldn't find. But though Perry was frequently searched and always under suspicion, he was never actually caught doing anything illegal.

So, was he or wasn't he? To this day nobody but Perry himself knows the truth.

Mind games and greaseballs aside, Gaylord Perry was an excellent pitcher over the course of his long career. He was a five-time All-Star and the first player to win the Cy Young Award in both the National and American Leagues.

One of Perry's career highlights with the Giants came on September 17, 1968, when he threw a no-hitter against the St. Louis Cardinals. Amazingly, the very next day, Cardinals pitcher Ray Washburn threw a no-hitter himself against the Giants!

Like most pitchers, however, Gaylord Perry was not known for his great hitting. In one particularly dreadful season early in his career, he got only 3 hits in 56 at bats for a pitiful .054 average.

Legend has it that one day Giants manager Alvin Dark told a reporter, "They'll put a man on the moon before Gaylord Perry hits a home run." Dark meant it as an off-hand joke—certainly not a prophecy—and his remark was soon forgotten.

However, it just so happens that a few years later, on July 20, 1969, the Giants were playing a day game against the Dodgers at Candlestick Park. Gaylord Perry was the starting pitcher but struggled early, giving up three runs in the first inning.

Meanwhile, more than 200,000 miles away, the Apollo 11 spacecraft was circling the moon. At 1:17 p.m. California time, the lunar module *Eagle*, carrying astronauts Neil Armstrong and Buzz Aldrin, touched down on the moon's surface in an area called the Sea of Tranquility. As the world waited in anxious anticipation, Armstrong reported back to Mission Control in Houston, "The Eagle has landed." For the first time ever, man had landed on the moon!

Back in San Francisco, Gaylord Perry stepped to the plate in the bottom of the third inning. There were already two outs, and the Giants were still losing, 3-0. Perry took three balls and then got a pitch to his liking. He swung, the ball flew over the fence, and Perry had finally done it. He'd hit his first-ever major league home run.

So, as it turns out, they did put a man on the moon before Gaylord Perry hit a home run. Alvin Dark was right about that—but only by a few minutes!

DAVE DRAVECKY'S MIRACLE COMEBACK

FROM THE TIME HE WAS eight years old, Dave Dravecky dreamed of playing major league baseball. He was a left-handed pitcher, so he idolized southpaw greats like Sandy Koufax and Vida Blue. Someday, he wanted to pitch just like them.

It took a lot of hard work to make that dream come true. After playing in high school and college, Dravecky was drafted in the 21st round. He pitched at every level of the minor leagues, making stops in Charleston, Buffalo, Amarillo, and even Hawaii. It all paid off when he finally took the mound for the San Diego Padres in June of 1982. He was a major leaguer at last.

After several good years in San Diego, Dravecky was traded to the San Francisco Giants in 1987. He immediately became a key member of the Giants' starting rotation, and the team clinched the division title.

Dravecky pitched brilliantly that fall in the National League Championship Series. He started two games against St. Louis and gave up only one run in 15 innings of work. But it wasn't enough. The Cardinals shut out the Giants in games 6 and 7 and went on to the World Series while Dave and his teammates went home.

At the start of the next season, Dravecky felt a pain in his pitching arm that wouldn't go away. He went to his doctor, who sent him to a hospital for x-rays and an MRI. Dave and his wife sat in the waiting room while the doctors looked at the test results. Then they heard someone say in a low voice, "Look at the tumor."

Later, the doctor sat down to talk to Dave and his wife Jan, and he confirmed their worst fears. Dave had cancer. The tumor was in the shoulder muscle of his left arm, and he would need to have surgery right away to prevent the cancer from spreading to other parts of his body.

Dravecky describes the months that followed as a "whirlwind of surgery, radiation, pain and depression." Surgeons removed half of his deltoid muscle and froze the humerus bone in his upper arm to try and kill all the cancer cells. The recovery was difficult and painful, and it seemed impossible to imagine that he would ever pitch again.

But Dave Dravecky refused to give up on the dream he'd had since he was eight years old. He desperately wanted to get back to pitching in the major leagues. So he worked hard despite the pain, fighting his way through grueling therapy sessions. His arm got stronger and stronger, and he was finally ready to try pitching again.

Against all odds, Dravecky returned to the majors on August 10, 1989 to start at home for the Giants against the Cincinnati Reds.

Dave and his family had been through a lot, so of course this start was a big deal for them. But they didn't realize how important it was for the thousands of fans who packed into Candlestick Park that day to welcome him back. Athletes battle back from injuries all the time, but coming back from the big C—CANCER— was something truly amazing. The fact that he not only survived, but had come back to pitch in the major leagues, seemed like a modern-day miracle.

Dravecky got a standing ovation from the fans when he started warming up in the bullpen. He got another ovation when he took the mound for the start of the game. Then he got a standing ovation when he retired the first three batters in the first inning. And so on.

Even the Giants manager, Roger Craig, admitted, "I didn't really manage that game. I just sat there in awe."

Just by taking the mound, Dravecky impressed the fans with his faith, courage and determination. And then he pitched one heck of a ballgame. He felt energized by the outpouring of support from the crowd, and the 4-0 lead provided by his teammates didn't hurt either. His control was nearly perfect. He held the Reds scoreless for most of the game before giving up a three-run homer in the eighth inning. After closer Steve "Bedrock" Bedrosian got the save in the ninth, the Giants had a 4-3 victory, and Dave Dravecky came out of the dugout for yet another standing ovation from the fans.

He had done it. He had won. He had triumphed over cancer and battled back to make his boyhood dreams come true. And he had inspired thousands of cancer patients around the world in their own struggles against that deadly opponent.

It seems like the story ought to end just like that: the triumphant hero celebrating with his jubilant teammates and fans. But, sadly, this story took a different turn.

Only five days later, Dravecky started his second

game, this time in Montreal against the Expos. He pitched well again and didn't give up any runs in the first five innings. But he started to feel a slight tingling sensation in his pitching arm. When he started the sixth inning, things got worse: he gave up a lead-off home run and then hit the next batter.

Then, as he threw his first pitch to batter Tim Raines, Dravecky heard an "incredible explosion" in his left ear. Fans in the stadium and watching on TV could also hear a loud crack as he delivered the pitch.

That crack was the sound of Dave's left arm breaking.

He crumpled to the ground, rolling around in agonizing pain much worse than anything he'd felt before. The other players rushed to the mound as fans in the stands watched in helpless horror.

The bone in his upper arm had been weakened when it was frozen to eliminate the cancer. It simply couldn't hold up to the stress and strain of pitching, so it eventually snapped.

After some unsuccessful surgeries, doctors discovered in 1991 that the cancer had returned. Dravecky's left arm and shoulder had to be amputated.

Dave faced many new challenges and frustrations adjusting to life with just one arm. But, just like before, he worked hard to overcome those obstacles, and now he and Jan have dedicated their lives to helping people who suffer from cancer and other illnesses.

Dave Dravecky learned there were more important things in life than baseball. Though his pitching career ended much too soon, Dravecky's story of hope and determination has proven far greater and more lasting than anything he ever could have imagined.

EARTHQUAKE!

DID YOU EVER HAVE ONE of those dreams where everything seems happy and wonderful at first, but then things take a nasty shift, and suddenly you're in the middle of an awful nightmare?

That's exactly how the 1989 season felt for Bay Area baseball fans.

Early in the year, the Giants had been picked to finish third or fourth in their division, but the team exceeded everyone's expectations. Kevin Mitchell clobbered 47 home runs and was named the National League MVP. He barely beat out his teammate Will Clark, who hit .333 with 23 home runs and 111 RBI. The infield played excellent defense, and pitcher Scott Garrelts had the league's lowest ERA (2.28). Ignited by the "Humm Baby" spirit of manager Roger Craig, the Giants seized first place in mid-June and led the NL West the rest of the season.

Meanwhile, just across the bay, the Oakland A's were having an excellent year themselves. They had lost the World Series to the Dodgers the year before and wanted another chance to win it all. Despite some early injuries to key players, including "Bash Brothers" Mark McGwire and Jose Canseco, the A's took the lead in the AL West and clinched their division title the same night the Giants did.

As the playoffs got underway, the Giants faced off against the Chicago Cubs in the National League Championship Series. Sweet-swinging first baseman Will Clark immediately showed why he'd earned the nickname "The Thrill." He set the tone in the very first game at Wrigley Field, going 4-for-4 with two home runs—including a grand slam—to lead the Giants to an 11-3 win.

The Cubs took Game 2 in Chicago, but the Giants came back to win the next two games at home, giving them a 3-1 lead in the series.

Game 5 would also be in San Francisco, and the Giants really wanted to clinch the pennant at home in front of their fans. Starting pitcher Rick "Big Daddy" Reuschel allowed the Cubs just one run in eight innings.

The Giants were held scoreless until the seventh, when Clark led off with a triple and then scored on a sacrifice fly to tie the game at 1-1.

Will Clark was in the spotlight again in the bottom of the eighth. After three consecutive walks, the Giants had the bases loaded with two outs, and Cubs closer Mitch "Wild Thing" Williams was coming in from the bullpen with the game on the line. This was the kind of moment Clark lived for. He fouled off one Williams fastball after another, the tension rising on each pitch, until he finally won the battle with a single to center field. Two runs crossed the plate, the home crowd exploded in celebration, and Giants radio broadcaster Hank Greenwald exclaimed, "Superman has done it again!"

San Francisco held on in the ninth inning to win the game, 3-2. For the first time in 27 years, the Giants were going to the World Series—a real "thrill" for the players and their fans!

Waiting for the Giants were their cross-bay rivals, the Oakland A's, who had also dominated their League Championship Series against the Toronto Blue Jays. Rickey Henderson, acquired by the A's midway through the season, had an amazing playoff series. He drove in five runs on six hits, walked seven times, and stole eight bases. Rickey seemed to be everywhere, and the havoc he created helped the A's easily defeat the Blue Jays in five games.

It was a dream come true for Northern California baseball fans. For the first time ever, the two teams on opposite sides of San Francisco Bay would face each other in the World Series.

Some fans were happy to root for both teams. They wore special caps that were half green-and-gold for the A's and half orange and black for the Giants. Everyone in the Bay Area felt proud and excited to have the whole world watching as their two teams battled for the championship.

The first two World Series games were played in Oakland and completely dominated by the Athletics. Their ace pitcher, the scowling Dave Stewart, pitched a complete-game shutout in Game 1, and the Giants managed just five hits as they lost 5-0. They didn't do much better against Game 2 starter Mike Moore, who gave up only four hits in a 5-1 Oakland win. The A's, who were determined to avenge their humiliating World Series loss the year before, seemed unstoppable.

Giants fans had to cling to the hope that when the team returned to their home field in San Francisco for Game 3, they could regain some momentum and start scoring some runs.

October 17, 1989, was a beautiful, unusually warm fall afternoon, even at notoriously chilly Candlestick Park. As fans filed into the stadium for the 5:30 p.m. game, everyone agreed that it was a perfect day for baseball.

Broadcasters from radio and TV stations around the world chatted about the first two games of the Series and how the Giants badly needed to win this one at home. Excited fans loaded up on hot dogs and drinks and started heading for their seats. The players began lining up on the field at 5:00 for pre-game ceremonies and introductions.

Four minutes later, disaster struck. It started with an incredible roar, like the sound of a massive jet flying overhead. Then everything began to shake. Down on the field, the sudden jolts almost knocked over some of the players. Giants pitcher (and future broadcaster) Mike Krukow said it felt like "a 600 pound gopher going underneath your feet at 43 miles per hour."

Of course, this was no gopher. It was an earthquake!

Up in the stands, the concrete beneath the seats rippled and rolled in ocean-like waves. Glass windows in the luxury boxes rattled, and the ballpark's huge light towers swayed wildly from side to side. Chunks of cement from the second deck fell onto the seats below.

If you live in California, you get used to the occasional quake. But this was no ordinary shaker.

A's pitcher Gene Nelson was sitting in the clubhouse while everything around him heaved violently. He said later, "I was absolutely sure the stadium was going to come down on me."

Incredibly, Candlestick did not crumble. After the rumbling and shaking finally stopped, there was a moment of stunned silence. Then some cheers and nervous laughter started to erupt from the crowd. The earthquake was over. They had survived!

Giants pitcher Atlee Hammaker joked: "I guess the momentum has shifted."

At first, fans wanted the game to go on. But the electricity had been knocked out by the quake, and it soon became clear that the ballpark would have to be evacuated quickly to get everyone out before darkness fell. Shaken spectators shuffled quietly to the exits.

Some fans had brought transistor radios or portable TVs, and as they listened to the news reports, they began to realize that the earthquake had caused much more serious problems outside the park.

A section of the Bay Bridge had collapsed, as had a freeway interchange in Oakland. Some people had been crushed in their cars, and many more were trapped in the rubble. Several buildings had caved in or crumbled, especially in the Marina District of San Francisco, where fires blazed through entire neighborhoods. The downtown areas of Santa Cruz and Watsonville, closer to the quake's epicenter, were almost completely destroyed. Throughout the region, paramedics, firefighters, police officers, and ordinary citizens rushed to rescue trapped victims and help the injured.

The Loma Prieta earthquake, as it was later named, measured 6.9 on the Richter scale. The biggest earthquake to hit Northern California since 1906, it killed 63 people, injured nearly 4,000 more, and left as many as 10,000 people homeless.

With such an enormous tragedy affecting so many lives, nobody knew quite what to do about the World Series. Some players thought the remaining games should be cancelled. "A lot of things are happening here that are more important than baseball," said Giants second baseman Robby Thompson.

But many people thought that baseball would help the community heal. After all the death and destruction, the Bay Area needed something to cheer about. And so, after a 10-day delay, the World Series finally resumed.

Everyone felt a little nervous and uncomfortable

returning to Candlestick for the long-awaited Game 3. The crowd was more subdued, and the players found it hard to focus. A moment of silence at 5:04 p.m. honored the people who had died in the earthquake, and the ceremonial first pitch was thrown out by emergency workers who had bravely helped during the disaster.

Once the baseball game finally started, things seemed almost back to normal. Unfortunately for the Giants, the A's picked up right where they had left off. The long delay meant that Oakland was able to start a well-rested Dave Stewart again, and he held the Giants to just three runs over the first seven innings. The A's sluggers, meanwhile, smashed five homers, and Oakland rolled to another easy win, 13-7.

It looked like the momentum hadn't shifted for the home team after all.

In Game 4, the A's got out to a 7-0 lead and appeared to be cruising. The Giants finally gave their fans something to cheer about when they rallied for two runs in the sixth and added four more in the seventh. But it was too little, too late. Oakland held on to win the game, 9-6, and claimed the title of World Series Champions.

The four-game sweep was the most lopsided defeat in World Series history. But the celebration in the A's dugout was a quiet one, and even the disappointed

Giants players and fans couldn't feel too upset. Losing a few baseball games just didn't seem very important compared to the truly devastating losses suffered by so many.

Now, more than twenty years later, people still remember the earthquake that brought the 1989 World Series to a halt. But they also celebrate the bravery and community spirit that brought the entire Bay Area together in the face of terrible tragedy.

SPLASH HIT:
A NEW BALLPARK IN CHINA BASIN

IT SEEMS HARD TO BELIEVE now, but there was a time when it looked like San Francisco fans were going to lose their Giants for good. It was 1992, and for many years, the team had been struggling, both on the field and at the box office. Fans hated Candlestick Park but had repeatedly rejected proposals to build a new ballpark.

After losing millions of dollars every year, owner Bob Lurie finally decided enough was enough. He agreed to sell to a group of investors who planned to move the team all the way to Florida. At the last game of the season, desperate Giants fans brought signs that said "WE'LL MISS YOU" and "PLEASE DON'T GO!"

But just when it seemed like the Giants were really and truly "outta here," they found another late-inning hero in local businessman and longtime Giants fan Peter Magowan.

As an eight-year-old boy growing up in New York, young Peter went to his first major league game at the Polo Grounds in 1950. From that day on, the Giants were his team. When he wasn't in the stands rooting for his favorite players, he had his ear glued to Russ Hodges' radio broadcasts. Peter and his classmates even convinced their teacher to let them listen to the playoff game in 1951 that ended in the "Shot Heard 'Round The World." It was a moment he would never forget.

So you can imagine the heartbreak Peter Magowan felt in 1958 when his beloved Giants packed up and left for California. "How could anybody take my Giants away from me?" he wondered.

Fortunately for Magowan, his family also moved from New York to San Francisco a short time later, so he never stopped rooting for the Giants. He never forgot what it felt like to lose his baseball team, either. So when the Giants seemed destined for Florida, he just couldn't sit by and watch the same thing happen to kids in the Bay Area. Peter Magowan worked day and night until he'd found local investors who were willing to put up enough cash to buy the team for $100 million.

They had saved the team for San Francisco. But

Magowan knew he still had one big problem to solve: the curse of Candlestick Park. The Bay Area had plenty of loyal baseball fans, but they were tired of the cold, windy conditions at the 'Stick, so they hadn't been coming to very many games. And it was hard for the team to sign new free-agent players because nobody wanted to play at the unpopular park.

Magowan also knew that the Giants couldn't depend on the city to build a new park for them. Voters had already rejected that idea four separate times. So he decided to try a different approach: he'd get large corporations and wealthy businessmen to help pay more than $250 million for a new state-of-the-art ballpark. No one had built a stadium without taxpayer money since the Dodgers did it in 1962, but Magowan believed he could make it work.

He was right. After many meetings with city leaders, architects, and engineers, the Giants decided to build their new ballpark next to the waterfront in a part of the city known as China Basin. At the time, the site didn't look like much. The run-down neighborhood was mostly dilapidated old concrete warehouses and abandoned pier buildings.

But the architects could see the site's enormous potential: it had great views of the water, the Bay Bridge, and the city skyline. It was close to downtown and to public transportation, making it easy for fans to walk or take the train to games. And although the site overlooked the bay, it was sheltered from the freezing cold winds that had made life at Candlestick so miserable.

After years of discussion and planning, construction finally got underway. And when the Giants opened the season in 2000, they took the field in a gleaming jewel of a park that is now the pride of San Francisco.

The ballpark in China Basin, originally named Pacific Bell Park, is now AT&T Park. But whatever you call it, the new stadium is truly a wonderful place to watch baseball. It was designed to feel like a classic old-time ballpark, but with modern comforts and conveniences. When you're there, you should take some time to explore all of its unique features, which include:

Hall of Famers Guarding the Gates

The Giants wanted to be sure that the team's long history remained part of their brand new ballpark. The main entrance is a tribute to the greatest Giant of them all: Willie Mays. The plaza features 24 palm trees (after Mays' uniform number 24) and a huge bronze statue of Willie himself, just finishing a mighty swing and looking up—probably watching one of his 660 home runs go "Bye, Bye, Baby." At other entrances to the park, you can find similar statues of Willie's teammates and fellow Hall of Famers, Orlando Cepeda and Juan Marichal.

Field of Dreams

Once you get inside, take a good look at the baseball field itself. Candlestick Park and most of the other big stadiums built in the 1960s and 70s had boring, symmetrical outfields. They all looked alike, and people called them "cookie cutter" stadiums.

But the new field's dimensions are very irregular, more like old-time ballparks. The first thing most players notice is the tempting short "porch" in right field: it's only 309 feet from home plate. But the wall is 24 feet high, so it's not as easy to hit a home run there as it looks. There are a couple of jagged corners in right center field where the grassy expanse stretches out to 421 feet. Balls hit into this gap often lead to extra bases, which is why it's earned the nickname "Triples Alley." The left field fence is at 339 feet but is only 8 feet tall. All these unusual dimensions add quirkiness to the park and make for a more interesting game.

There's also not very much foul territory, which means that spectators are right on top of the action.

In fact, the lucky fans who sit behind home plate are actually closer to the batter than the pitcher is!

Giant Playground

The owners wanted to be sure that the ballpark was a fun place for kids, even those who are too young to really follow the game itself. So the area behind left field is designated the Fan Lot, where kids can play while their parents keep an eye on the ballgame.

The most distinctive feature is the 80-foot Coke bottle, with several long twisty slides inside. Next to that is a giant 26-foot-tall baseball glove, modeled after an old-fashioned four-finger glove. Made out of steel and fiberglass, it is carefully sculpted to look like broken-in old leather, with real marine rope for the stitching.

There's also a miniature baseball field where kids can bat and run the bases just like their major league idols. And over behind center field is a real cable car where you can ring the bell or just sit and watch the game. But sorry, L.A. fans. According to the sign, there are "NO DODGER FANS ALLOWED."

The Cove

Out past the right field wall is an area known as the Portwalk. Because it runs directly next to the water, it had to be kept open to the public. The park designers decided to include open archways in the right field wall so that people walking by could peek in and watch the game from outside—for free!

Beyond the Portwalk are the waters of McCovey Cove, named for the Giants' beloved first baseman. And watching over the Cove is a towering statue of Willie Mac himself.

It doesn't happen often, but if you're lucky you'll see a batter hit a ball so hard that it soars over the right field wall, clears the Portwalk, and plops into the water: a Splash Hit!

On game days, you'll find the Cove filled with people in boats and kayaks, soaking up the sunshine and hoping to catch a home run ball. It's something you can only see in San Francisco at the Giants' unique and beautiful ballpark.

FOLLOWING IN GIANT FOOTSTEPS

A PROMISING YOUNG PLAYER named Bobby Bonds got called up by the Giants for a home game against the Dodgers in June 1968. It didn't take long for him to announce his arrival. In his third at bat, Bonds got his first hit in the major leagues: a grand-slam home run!

One of the players who scored on that first big blast was Willie Mays, who was then nearing the end of his Hall of Fame career. Willie thought Bobby was a lot like himself at a younger age. He liked the fact that Bonds was eager to learn and asked lots of questions about the game. Mays soon became a mentor to the young rookie and helped him adjust to life in the major leagues.

Bobby Bonds quickly developed into a star outfielder for the Giants. In 1969 he became only the second

National League player (after Mays) to hit 30 home runs and steal 30 bases in a season. Bobby was the first person to do that five times in his career, a feat matched by only one player since. Can you guess who that might be? (If not, you'll soon find out!)

Bobby Bonds had an unusual combination of power and speed. He was also an excellent fielder with a strong arm. Many Giants fans thought he had the potential to be the next Willie Mays. Bobby felt honored by the comparison; he once described Mays as "the greatest player to ever wear shoes." In fact, he admired Mays so much that he asked Willie to be the honorary godfather for his young son, Barry.

Though flattering, the comparisons to Mays also put a lot of pressure on Bobby Bonds, who never quite lived up to the high expectations everyone had for him. After seven years with the Giants, Bonds was traded, and he spent the rest of his career moving from team to team. Still, he finished with 332 home runs, 461 stolen bases, three Gold Glove awards and three appearances in the All-Star game—a stellar baseball career most people could only dream about.

Meanwhile, Bobby's son Barry grew up hanging out in the clubhouse with his dad and godfather and other big league ballplayers. Barry himself was a very talented athlete who excelled in football, basketball, and baseball in high school. He was good enough to be drafted by the Giants after he graduated, but he decided to go to college and play baseball at Arizona State University instead. He was then drafted by the Pittsburgh Pirates and soon became a rising young star.

When Barry started his major league career, Bobby Bonds told his old friend and teammate, Orlando Cepeda, "My son's going to be one of the greatest players of all time." Orlando chuckled and told Bobby, "All fathers say that." Before long, though, it became clear that Bobby wasn't just another proud dad bragging about his kid.

Barry Bonds played for seven years for the Pirates, quickly gaining fame as one of the elite players in the National League. In 1990 he joined his father and godfather in the 30-30 club when he hit 33 homers and stole 52 bases. That year he was named to the All-Star team and won his first MVP award. Bonds led the Pirates to the National League East division title three years in a row, but the team never made it all the way to the World Series.

Following another MVP season in 1992, Barry became a free agent, which meant he could sign with any team. He thought he might go to the New York

Yankees. But at the same time, back in San Francisco, Peter Magowan was trying to put together a deal to buy the Giants and keep them from moving to Florida. He and his partners wanted to sign a big star who could be the centerpiece of the team. In a bold and risky move, the group approached Bonds and agreed to sign him for a record six-year $43 million contract—before they'd even officially taken ownership of the team!

Barry was very happy to sign with the Giants, and not just because of the big paycheck. For him, it was like coming home again. But playing for San Francisco meant that he had to choose a new uniform number. In Pittsburgh he'd worn number 24 in honor of Willie Mays, but that number had already been retired by the Giants. So Barry chose to wear number 25, which had been his dad's old number.

Bobby himself got to put on a Giants jersey again when the new owners hired him as a hitting instructor for the team. Willie Mays served as a special assistant for the Giants, so he and Bobby got to work together again. The Giants also hired Dusty Baker, a childhood pal of Bobby's, to manage the team. Together these old friends watched with pride as Barry became the best player in the major leagues.

For all his achievements on the field, Barry Bonds

was a quiet, reserved man who was often uncomfortable with reporters and broadcasters. But he was thrust into the national spotlight in 2001 when he began to stalk the single-season home run record. He set such a blistering pace early in the season that people began to believe he had a real chance at breaking Mark McGwire's record of 70 home runs in a season.

As the season went on, the front pages of Bay Area newspapers included a "Bonds Watch" to track his mounting home run total. National sports broadcasts led off with highlights of Barry's exploits. And everywhere the Giants played, fans packed the stadiums, hoping to see Bonds as he steadily slugged his way toward the record. Amazingly, it seemed that in almost every game, Barry would crush another one.

Or two. In fact, on the night Bonds hit the record-breaking 71st homer as camera flashes winked like fireflies at Pacific Bell Park, he followed it up with another fence-clearing shot in his very next at bat. Bonds ended the 2001 season with 73 home runs, a record that may never be broken.

Barry was more than just a slugger, though. Like only his father before him, he also hit at least 30 homers and stole 30 bases five times in his career. He eventually became the first (and so far the only) player to have more than 500 home runs and 500 steals in his lifetime. And he backed up his great hitting with outstanding defensive play, earning eight Gold Glove awards as a left fielder.

The list of eye-popping statistics goes on and on, but perhaps this is the most impressive: Barry Bonds was named the Most Valuable Player in the league seven times in his career. That's more than twice as many as any other player in all of baseball history!

Though he had never thought of himself as a home run hitter, Barry began slowly climbing the all-time record board. In 2001, on his way to breaking the single-season record, he became the 17th player to hit 500 career home runs. Soon he passed Mel Ott, the original Giants slugger, at 511. Two weeks later, he passed another Giants legend, Willie McCovey, at 521.

Bobby Bonds was no longer a hitting coach for the team, but he could always be found in the stands at Pacific Bell Park, cheering for Barry and the Giants.

Unfortunately, Bobby was also battling serious health problems. In 2002, he had to have surgery to remove a tumor from his kidney. But he was still there to celebrate with his son and the rest of the hometown fans when Barry passed the 600 home run mark. The only players ahead of him now were Willie Mays (660),

Babe Ruth (714), and Hank Aaron (755).

Barry kept hitting homers and marching toward milestones, but sadly, his father would not be there to see them all. After a long fight against lung cancer, pneumonia, and a brain tumor, Bobby Bonds died in August 2003.

Barry was devastated by the loss of his father, mentor, and friend. But he somehow managed to channel his sorrow into even more amazing baseball feats. Now, when he hit a home run, he would point heavenward as a way of honoring his father's memory.

In 2004, Bonds hit number 660 to tie his godfather. In an emotional moment, Willie Mays presented Barry with a ceremonial Olympic torch, proudly passing on a legacy of greatness to his beloved godson.

One thing that made Bonds' assault on the home run record even more incredible is that he didn't get very many good pitches to hit. Pitchers threw very carefully to Bonds. Managers often chose to walk him on purpose, even with other runners on base, rather than give him a chance to hit one out of the park.

It got so bad that Giants fans started waving rubber chickens every time Bonds was given a free pass, mocking opponents for being afraid to pitch to their star. Barry's young daughters came to games holding signs that read "PLEASE PITCH TO OUR DADDY!" But nobody wanted to pitch to Barry. And so, along with all his other achievements, Bonds also holds the major league records for both walks and intentional walks.

Finally, in 2007, Barry Bonds broke the one record that nobody, except maybe his father, had thought possible: Hank Aaron's 755 career home runs. Barry hit the record-breaker on August 7, 2007, against pitcher Mike Bacsik of the Washington Nationals. It was a towering shot that soared over the wall in deep right center field. As soon as he made contact, Barry knew he'd broken the record. He dropped his bat and raised his arms in triumph (and a little bit of relief too) before starting his run around the bases.

Though Bobby Bonds couldn't be there with his son on this historic moment, Willie Mays was waiting at home plate with a hug. And the San Francisco fans— as they had done so many times before for Willie, for Bobby, and for Barry—stood and cheered.

Like his father and his godfather before him, Barry Bonds had proven himself one of baseball's true Giants.

NEAR MISSES

NOBODY EVER SAID IT WAS EASY being a Giants fan. Throughout the team's long history, there have been close calls, spectacular seasons, outstanding individual performances, and many memorable moments. But ever since the team moved to San Francisco, they repeatedly fell short of the ultimate prize: a World Series championship. The Giants were often contenders, but even their best seasons always seemed to end in heartbreak.

1993: The Last Great Pennant Race

Under new manager Dusty Baker, the Giants won more than 100 games in 1993. The team had solid starting pitching; a reliable infield trio of Will Clark, Robby Thompson, and Matt Williams; and new offensive power from the bat of Barry Bonds.

The Atlanta Braves played all the way across the country but (for confusing reasons) were still part of the National League West division. And, unfortunately for the Giants, the Braves were also putting together a season for the record books. The teams battled back and forth throughout August and September. Every day, fans from San Francisco and Atlanta would check the box scores for both teams to see where they were in the standings.

Going into the last weekend of the season, the Giants and Braves were tied with 101 wins apiece. For the final series, the Giants would have to face their arch-rival Dodgers in Los Angeles. The Braves, meanwhile, would play at home against the expansion-team Rockies.

The Braves and Giants both won on Friday night. And both teams won again on Saturday. So the whole season came down to the last day. If both teams won, they'd have to play a one-game playoff to decide the pennant. But if only one team won, they would be the NL West Champions.

Atlanta played their game first and beat the Rockies 5-3, so the Giants knew they had to win to stay alive.

Thousands of Braves fans stayed at the ballpark in Atlanta to watch the Giants-Dodgers game broadcast live from L.A. on the scoreboard. To their delight, they saw the Giants' stellar season end in a complete train wreck.

Los Angeles grabbed a quick 3-0 lead against Giants rookie starter Salomon Torres. After a shaky Torres left the game in the fourth inning, the Dodgers continued to pummel the rest of the San Francisco pitching staff. In all, seven pitchers combined to give up 12 runs, including two homers by L.A. catcher Mike Piazza. Meanwhile, the Giants' offense, which had been so impressive all season, could only put up one measly run, and the Dodgers romped to a ridiculously easy win.

Just like that, in rather humiliating fashion, the Giants' dreams were dashed. They had won a remarkable 103 games, more than any other team in baseball except for the Braves. But their season was over.

In 1995, Major League Baseball introduced a new playoff format, giving the second-place team with the most wins in each league a "wild-card" berth in the playoffs. In some ways the new format is more fair to teams like those 1993 Giants. And in later years San Francisco would benefit from the new system. But many longtime baseball fans miss the kind of intense drama that gripped the whole nation in what is now remembered as the "last great pennant race."

1997: The Brian Johnson Game

The Giants found themselves in a battle for the 1997 division title with—who else?—the Los Angeles Dodgers. After a second-half slump, the Giants fought hard to get back into the lead. But on September 17, with less than two weeks left in the season, the Dodgers led by two games as they came to San Francisco for a two-game series. For both teams, this was crunch time.

Barry Bonds hit a two-run homer to power the Giants to victory in the series opener. The Dodgers' lead was down to just one game.

The next day, San Francisco fans packed the house to see if the Giants could do it again. Bonds delivered another homer, and so did first baseman J.T. Snow. It looked like the Giants might cruise to an easy win. But then the Dodgers fought back to tie it up, 5-5, and sent the game into extra innings.

In the top of the tenth, the Giants' ace closer, Rod Beck, gave up three consecutive singles. The Dodgers had the bases loaded with no outs. Dusty Baker visited the mound but decided to let Beck stay in the game.

"You're the guy," Baker told him.

The veteran pitcher, famous for his bushy mustache and intimidating stare, rewarded his manager's faith. Beck struck out the next batter, and then got pinch hitter Eddie Murray to ground into an unusual double play that nailed the runners at home and first. The Dodgers' rally was squashed, and the gut-wrenching game went on.

Two tense innings later, in the bottom of the twelfth, Giants catcher Brian Johnson blasted his way into team folklore. A local kid who had gone to high school in Oakland and played baseball and football at nearby Stanford University, Johnson became a Giants legend when he drilled the first pitch over the left field fence for a walk-off home run.

With that one swing of the bat, Johnson had given San Francisco the win, pulled them into a tie with L.A., and shifted the momentum of the division race back to the Giants. All the players ran onto the field to celebrate the dramatic victory. For the 50,000 fans who were there to see it, the moment was every bit as exciting as Bobby Thomson's home run back in 1951.

The stirring triumph now known simply as "the Brian Johnson game" propelled the Giants to the 1997 division title. But their hopes of making it to the World Series were squelched in the first round of the playoffs by the wild-card Florida Marlins, who swept the Giants in three straight games on their way to the World Series championship.

Giants pitcher Roberto Hernandez summed up the feelings of his teammates when he said, "It was fun… but the ride ended too quick. Much too quick."

2002: Death by Rally Monkey

The Giants themselves were the wild-card team in 2002, and they were determined to get all the way to the World Series this time. Barry Bonds had another fantastic season and won his fifth MVP award. Batting behind him in the lineup was second baseman Jeff Kent, who hit 37 homers and knocked in 108 runs. The two perennial All-Stars powered the Giants to 95 wins in the regular season.

But what Bonds, Kent, and the rest of the Giants really wanted was to wear the diamond rings of World Series Champions.

As the wild-card team, the Giants faced the Braves in the first round of the playoffs and squeaked by them, three games to two. Then they convincingly defeated the St. Louis Cardinals, four games to one, with a dramatic bottom-of-the-ninth victory in Game 5 to take the National League pennant. For the first time in 13 years, the Giants were back in the World Series.

Their opponents would be the Anaheim Angels, who had also fought their way through the playoffs as the wild-card team from the American League.

The 2002 World Series opened at Edison Field in Anaheim, California. The crowd of more than 44,000 red-clad Angels fans created a deafening roar by pounding on inflatable plastic "ThunderStix." And the entire stadium seemed to erupt when videos of the team's famous "Rally Monkey" (an actual Capuchin monkey wearing a mini Angels uniform) played on the scoreboard video screen.

Somehow, in the midst of all the mayhem, the Giants got down to business. With homers from Barry Bonds, Reggie Sanders, and J.T. Snow, the Giants silenced the Angels and their screeching rally monkey for a 4-3 win in Game 1.

The home run derby continued in a high-scoring Game 2, with the Angels prevailing for an 11-10 victory. Back in San Francisco, the Angels pounded the Giants in Game 3 for a 10-4 defeat, but the "G-Men" responded with a 4-3 win in Game 4 to tie the series at two games apiece.

In Game 5, the Giants played like champions. They scored three runs in the first inning and three more in the second, and they didn't stop there. Jeff Kent hit two home runs, and shortstop Rich Aurilia added another as the Giants cruised to an easy 16-4 win, one of the most lopsided games ever in a World Series.

The night's biggest drama came when Darren Baker, the three-year-old son of skipper Dusty Baker, trotted out from the Giants dugout to retrieve the bat of Kenny Lofton. Darren was so excited that he didn't realize the ball was still in play. Fortunately, as J.T. Snow sprinted home on Lofton's triple, he scooped up Darren at the plate and pulled him to safety just before David Bell barreled home behind him. After the game, Snow explained, "He's our good-luck charm. We can't afford to lose him."

Heading back to Anaheim with a 3-2 series lead, the Giants only needed one more win to claim their first World Series title in nearly 50 years. They could almost taste the champagne.

Game 6 was scoreless through the first four innings. Then the Giants broke through with home runs from Shawon Dunston and Barry Bonds (who batted an astounding .471 for the Series). San Francisco had a commanding 5-0 lead midway through the seventh.

After the Angels got two consecutive singles off Giants starter Russ Ortiz, manager Dusty Baker decided it was time to pull Ortiz and bring in a relief pitcher from the bullpen. Baker felt so sure that the team would hold on to the 5-0 lead that he flipped the game ball to Ortiz. He wanted the pitcher to save it as a souvenir of what looked like a sure World Series victory.

The Angels noticed Dusty's gesture—and they didn't appreciate it much. As the rally monkey shrieked and bounced on the Jumbotron, sending the Anaheim fans into a frenzy, the Angels roared back to score three runs in the seventh and three more in the eighth. The shell-shocked Giants ended up losing, 6-5.

There was still one game to play, but the spirit of the Giants seemed to have been crushed by the devastating loss. After having scored 43 runs in the first six games of the series, they could muster just a single run in Game 7. Starting pitcher Livan Hernandez gave up four runs to the Angels in the first three innings, and that was the ballgame. The listless Giants lost 4-1, and the World Series was over.

Once again, despite a great season and many exciting moments, the Giants and their fans had fallen just short of their dreams. They still had not won a World Series in San Francisco.

TORTURE

"GIANTS BASEBALL: TORTURE!"

Giants broadcaster Duane Kuiper coined this slogan early in the 2010 season, after the team barely escaped with a narrow win over the Astros on May 15. The game had been a tense pitchers' duel, with the Giants clinging to a 2-1 lead going into the ninth inning. Giants closer Brian Wilson came in from the bullpen hoping to get three quick outs to secure the victory.

Unfortunately, Wilson walked the very first batter. But then he got two quick outs, so 40,000 fans at AT&T Park rose to their feet, ready to celebrate. Instead, they had to wait, squirming anxiously, while Wilson gave up a single and then another walk. Suddenly, the Astros had the bases loaded!

Wilson promptly got two strikes on the next hitter,

111

and again the crowd roared in anticipation of the final out. But it wasn't over yet. The batter refused to give in, fouling off one pitch after another.

The hometown crowd was in agony, but Wilson himself wasn't nervous at all. He actually relished this kind of pressure. And he came through, finally ending the battle after 15 grueling pitches with a harmless fly ball to left. The Giants got the 2-1 win, and the fans went home feeling both exhilarated and exhausted at the same time.

This wasn't the first time the 2010 Giants had made their faithful followers endure this kind of nerve-wracking torture, and it certainly wouldn't be the last. In fact, the entire season was a thrilling journey that will forever be remembered by San Francisco fans.

So come along for the ride—if you think you've got the stomach for it!

Regular Season Rollercoaster

Throughout the regular season, the Giants' pitching was the backbone of the team. The starting rotation was built around a "homegrown" core: two-time Cy Young Award winner Tim "The Freak" Lincecum, dependable workhorse Matt Cain, lefty Jonathan Sanchez, and rookie Madison Bumgarner, who joined the team in June. They combined with veteran Barry Zito and a host of reliable relievers to post a league-best 3.36 ERA.

The offense, however, tended to be unpredictable. As a result, the team yo-yoed up and down in the division standings, sometimes getting hot and winning three or four games in a row, but then slumping and falling behind again.

San Francisco finished the first half of the season stuck in fourth place with a 41-40 record. It was the Fourth of July, and as fireworks filled the sky, nobody knew that the Giants were about to catch fire themselves.

With some exciting new players in the lineup, including rookie catcher Buster Posey and veteran Pat "The Bat" Burrell, the energized Giants surged to a 20-8 record in July as they leapfrogged both the Rockies and Dodgers in the standings.

The club had found a winning formula, and only the San Diego Padres were ahead of them now. Could the Giants track them down before the season ran out?

Patiently Pursuing the Padres

In the build-up to a critical three-game series against the Padres in early August, pitcher Jonathan Sanchez made a bold pronouncement:

"We are going to make the playoffs."

"We are going to play San Diego now and we're going to beat them three times," he continued. "And if we get to first place, we're not going to look back."

Sanchez was brash. He was confident. He was not afraid to stir up the San Diego fans. And, unfortunately for the Giants, he was wrong.

In fact, the team lost two of three to the Padres in that series and spiraled downward in the standings throughout most of August. When even the usually dependable starting pitchers began to struggle, Giants fans wondered if it was going to be yet another "wait 'til next year" kind of season.

By late August, San Diego had built a commanding 6½ game lead in the NL West. But the Giants and their fans refused to give up. Manager Bruce Bochy continued to shuffle his lineup in search of a more potent offense. Meanwhile, the team's front office picked up veteran Cody Ross before the Padres could claim him, even though it seemed the last thing the Giants needed was another outfielder.

In September, the starting pitchers regained their dominance, and bullpen hurlers Brian Wilson and Sergio Romo grew thick black beards that made them look like fearsome pirates. First baseman Aubrey Huff, a veteran player who was very focused on the field but a bit of a goofball in the clubhouse, started wearing red sequined underwear, claiming the "rally thong" would bring the team luck.

Who knows? Maybe it did. For somehow, magically, all of these factors combined to create a new energy and enthusiasm in the team. To the delight of their loyal fans, the Giants slowly but surely fought their way back into the race for the NL West.

They went 18-8 in September and gave themselves a comfortable three-game lead over San Diego going into the final weekend, when they would be playing at home against the Padres themselves. All the Giants had to do was win one game out of three, and they'd be in the playoffs for the first time since 2003.

But you didn't really think it would be that easy, did you? Of course not.

Instead, as had been their style all season, the Giants made it dramatic. They lost the first game on Friday night. Then they lost again on Saturday. Their lead had dwindled to just one game, and it all came down to the last day of the regular season.

Taking the hill for the Giants would be Jonathan Sanchez, the man who had boldly predicted back in August that the Giants would win the division.

This time, he was right.

Standing tall on the mound, Sanchez kept the Padres off balance through five scoreless innings. He had a big day at the plate, too, hitting his first career triple and scoring the game's first run. That was all his team would need as the bullpen completed the shutout and the Giants won, 3-0, to claim their ticket to the postseason.

As the players celebrated on the field, the fans drew a huge sigh of relief. It hadn't been pretty, but the Giants had made it to the playoffs!

Bring on the Braves

The torture would continue as the Giants faced the injury-hobbled Atlanta Braves in the best-of-five National League West Division Series.

Tim Lincecum was simply untouchable in the opening game, striking out 14 batters and giving up just two hits in a complete-game 1-0 victory.

In Game 2, Matt Cain also pitched brilliantly, and the Giants were ahead 4-1 going into the eighth. But the bullpen blew the lead, the game went into extra innings, and the Giants ended up losing, 5-4. So the series was tied as the teams headed back to Atlanta, home of the legendary tomahawk-chopping fans at Turner Field.

Game 3 of the series was a wild and messy affair. In the ninth inning, with two outs and the score tied 2-2, the Giants got a little help from Braves' second baseman Brooks Conrad, who had already made two errors. Buster Posey hit a sharp ground ball that skipped through Conrad's legs for his record third error of the game, allowing the Giants to score the go-ahead run. Even die-hard Giants fans had to feel sorry for the guy. Posey himself said afterwards, "You don't ever wish that upon somebody." But the team was happy to take the 3-2 win.

Game 4 in Atlanta was a hard-fought pitching battle between Braves starter Derek Lowe and Giants rookie Madison Bumgarner. Lowe was working on a no-hitter until Cody Ross finally broke through with a home run in the sixth inning. Ross and the Giants managed to scrape together two more runs in the seventh, and they had a 3-2 lead as the Braves came up for their last turn at bat.

The jet-black bearded Wilson came in for the save but (to nobody's surprise at this point) made it thrilling right to the end. Wilson walked two batters to put the tying and winning runs aboard before finally getting the last two outs to end the inning and clinch the first-round series for the Giants.

No Fear in Philly

The Giants now had to face the intimidating Philadelphia Phillies, who appeared to be steamrolling toward their third straight National League pennant. Philadelphia's top three starting pitchers were considered by many to be the best in baseball, and they also had a deep lineup of dangerous hitters. The Phillies seemed destined to get back to the World Series, which they had won just two years earlier.

The Giants, meanwhile, had a scrappy band of youngsters, oddballs, and castoffs who were, frankly, delighted to have made it this far. It had been a great ride, and if it had to end here, well, the San Francisco fans certainly had enjoyed all the fun.

But the Giants' weird and wonderful season wasn't over yet.

In Game 1, Cody Ross continued his hot streak at the plate, homering not just once but twice in his first two at bats against the mighty Roy Halladay. The Giants held on for a 4-3 win.

In Game 2, Cody Ross hit yet another home run, but that was the only score the Giants could muster against veteran pitcher Roy Oswalt in a humbling 6-1 loss that shifted the momentum back to the Phillies.

Matt Cain quickly reversed the tide when the teams

returned to San Francisco for Game 3. He threw seven superb shutout innings to help the Giants defeat the Phillies, 3-0. The underdogs had struck again and had a 2-1 lead in the series!

Game 4 was the kind of thriller that Giants fans had come to expect by this time. The box score bounced around like a bobblehead doll: the Giants went up 2-0, then fell down 4-2, then went back up 5-4 before surrendering the tying run in the eighth inning.

The score was still knotted at 5-5 as San Francisco came to bat in the ninth. Huff and Posey sent back-to-back singles into right field. With runners at first and third, the table was set for Juan Uribe, who had been kept out of the starting lineup with an injured wrist. He promptly delivered a deep drive to left for a walk-off sacrifice fly that gave the Giants the win and a 3-1 edge in the series.

After this thrilling win, centerfielder Andres Torres said the only problem he had was figuring out which of the game's many stars he should congratulate first: "I went to everybody," he explained afterwards. "I tried to hug everybody."

The Phillies fought back and won Game 5 by a score of 4-2 to stay alive in the series. Still, the Giants needed just one more win as the teams returned to Philadelphia.

Manager Bruce Bochy pulled out all the stops in a nerve-wracking Game 6. Jonathan Sanchez gave up two quick runs in the first, and he barely made it into the third inning before giving way to a parade of relievers. Bochy ordered just about every available arm to the mound, including starters Bumgarner and Lincecum. His maneuvers paid off as the staff combined to shut down the Phillies the rest of the way.

Meanwhile, the Giants pushed across two runs in the third inning to tie the game at 2-2. The teams remained deadlocked until the eighth, when Juan Uribe became a hero again. He blasted a huge opposite-field home run to put San Francisco ahead, 3-2.

But the Giants couldn't celebrate yet. They still needed closer Brian Wilson to preserve that slim one-run lead. And Wilson made it exciting. In the bottom of the ninth, he walked one batter, then walked another. But when he got Phillies slugger Ryan Howard to stare at a called strike three, Giants fans finally got to cheer: "We're going to the World Series!"

Wrangling the Rangers

The Giants hadn't won the World Series since 1954, back when the team still played in New York. And the Texas Rangers had never even been to the Fall Classic.

At the start of the season, nobody in the baseball world would have picked these two teams to match up in the World Series.

But now fans in both San Francisco and Arlington were wild with joy and anticipation. Giants diehards packed the stands at AT&T Park for Game 1 wearing bright orange shirts, stringy Lincecum wigs, and all manner of fake black beards. They waved red rally thongs and signs that warned "FEAR THE BEARD" while they rocked out to the team's unofficial anthem, Journey's "Don't Stop Believing."

Game 1 of the World Series promised to be a taut battle between two of the most dominating pitchers in baseball. Lincecum was matched up against Rangers ace Cliff Lee, who had been lights-out in postseason play.

But almost from the very beginning, the game was an offensive shootout. The score was tied 2-2 when the Giants erupted for six more runs in the fifth inning. Second baseman Freddy Sanchez doubled in his first three World Series at bats (the first player ever in history to do so), and Juan Uribe continued his long-ball exploits with a three-run homer. The Rangers put some runs on the board too, but the Giants outslugged them and won 11-7.

In Game 2, it was Matt Cain's turn to shine. The

steady right-hander, often overshadowed by his more colorful teammates, quietly went to work and completely shut down the Rangers' big bats. Cain threw 7⅔ more shutout innings to keep his postseason ERA at a remarkable 0.00.

San Francisco had just a slim 2-0 lead after seven innings, but once the Texas bullpen took over, the Giants restarted their offensive machine with a stunning two-out rally in the bottom of the eighth inning. For the raucous crowd in San Francisco, the torture turned to laughter as the Giants racked up a 9-0 lead and romped to another surprisingly drama-free win.

Heading to Arlington for Game 3, the Giants had a comfortable two-game lead in the Series but knew the Rangers weren't going to go down that easy. And sure enough, the Texas team gave their hometown fans something to cheer about, beating the Giants 4-2.

Game 4 happened to fall on Halloween night, and throughout the Bay Area, Giants fans were glued to their TVs, radios, laptops, and mobile phones to keep track of the game even while out trick-or-treating.

The Giants started Madison Bumgarner, who was only 21 years old (and probably had been trick-or-treating himself only a few years earlier). But the rookie showed remarkable poise for a youngster, staying cool in the bright spotlight and holding the Rangers scoreless through eight innings. In the ninth, Brian Wilson came in with a four-run lead—and simply mowed down the Rangers, 1-2-3. It wasn't torture at all. The Giants cruised to a 4-0 victory and were now just one win away from the championship!

Lincecum and Lee matched up once again in Game 5, and this time fans got the tense, low-scoring affair they'd expected in the first game of the Series. Both pitchers had excellent command, and the game was still scoreless going into the seventh inning.

Then the Giants struck one final blow.

Once again, it was Cody Ross who led the assault. He grounded a sharp single to center field, and then Juan Uribe followed with his own line single. Huff advanced both runners with a sacrifice bunt, but Lee got Burrell to strike out swinging for the second out.

Up next: veteran shortstop Edgar Renteria. The 34-year-old Renteria had missed most of the 2010 season due to various injuries and was already thinking about retiring after the season. But he was no stranger to pressure-packed situations. Back in 1997, a much younger Renteria had been the hero for the Florida Marlins, hitting a dramatic game-winning single in extra innings to clinch a Game 7 World Series victory.

This time, batting for the Giants in the glare of the Texas lights, Renteria launched Lee's third pitch into deep left-center field. The ball carried just enough to sail over the outfield wall for a three-run home run that gave the Giants the lead and, ultimately, a 3-1 win and the World Series victory.

The torture was over, replaced by pure joy.

While dejected Rangers fans filed out of the stadium, the ecstatic Giants players stayed to celebrate with their teammates and loyal backers who had made the trip to Texas. Meanwhile, back in San Francisco, fans poured into the streets, honking horns, hugging strangers, and dancing wildly through the night.

World Champions at Last

Two days later, tens of thousands of fans from all over Northern California crowded into the city for a parade to welcome home their Giants.

Their World Champion San Francisco Giants. Fans in the Bay Area had waited 52 years to say those words. Some of them even remembered the first Giants parade down Montgomery and Market Streets back in 1958, when the team moved to the west coast and brought major league baseball to California.

Since that first parade, the San Francisco Giants had

provided their fans with so many thrills: Hall of Fame players, tight pennant races, record-breaking home runs, exciting victories, and heartbreaking losses. But through all the years, they'd always fallen just short of the ultimate prize. The glorious "torture" that their fans endured in 2010 was in a way symbolic of the team's entire history in San Francisco.

But now, thanks to this band of "castoffs and misfits," a team of talented freaks, underappreciated veterans, surprisingly mature rookies, and unlikely heroes, the Giants had brought the World Series trophy home to San Francisco.

At the end of the victory parade, amid all the orange-and-black pandemonium, rookie catcher Buster Posey stepped to the microphone and addressed the delirious crowd that had gathered at the Civic Center.

"Let's enjoy this today, tomorrow, for a week, maybe even a month," said Posey calmly.

"Then let's get back to work and make another run at it," he exclaimed, pounding the podium confidently and promising a bright future for the World Champion San Francisco Giants and their fans everywhere.

BACK FROM THE BRINK

HUNTER PENCE WAS NOT ready to go home yet.

He had only been a San Francisco Giant for a few months, but Pence loved his new teammates. He loved baseball. And he wanted to keep playing.

Unfortunately, the Giants had lost the first two games of the 2012 playoffs to the Reds, and if they lost again, their season would be over.

So before the critical win-or-go-home Game 3 in Cincinnati, Hunter Pence gathered his teammates in the dugout. As the players huddled in a tight circle around him, he started screaming furiously. "Get in here! Everyone get in here!" he yelled. "Look into each other's eyes! This is the most fun, the best team I have ever been on, and no matter what happens, we must not give in!"

With his voice rising and his bright blue eyes bugging out, Pence continued: "I want one more day with you! Win each moment, win each inning—it's all we have left! We owe it to each other! Play for each other!"

Pence's fiery speech was wild, and it was weird. It wasn't the type of thing you usually hear in a baseball dugout.

But it worked. The Giants listened. And when they took the field, they weren't playing for the money or the fame. They weren't playing to win a trophy or a ring. Instead, this group of 25 professional athletes came together as one team and simply played for each other.

The Giants won that game. Then they won the next game, and the game after that. And they didn't give up until they'd claimed their second World Series Championship in three years.

For the San Francisco Giants and their fans, winning the World Series was just as sweet the second time around. But what made the 2012 championship extra-special was not just the fact that the Giants won. It was how they won. Or, even more importantly, how they absolutely, positively, refused to lose.

After "Preacher" Pence's inspirational speech rallied the team in Cincinnati, the Giants won three straight games on the road to win the Division

Series — something no team in National League history had ever done before.

Next, the Giants moved on to face the St. Louis Cardinals in the National League Championship Series. But again the Giants fell behind quickly. The Cardinals jumped out to a 3-1 lead in the seven-game series, and the Giants found themselves in an all-too-familiar place.

Once more, their backs were against the wall. They had to win three elimination games in a row against the defending World Series champions. Even the most faithful Giants fans knew the chances of survival were very, very slim.

But slim odds are better than no odds at all. And the Giants found a way to beat those odds — and the Cardinals. Once again, they came together as a team, stringing together three straight season-saving victories to claim the National League pennant and another trip to the World Series.

And when they got to the World Series? Some wondered if they even had a chance against the Detroit Tigers, whose lineup included some of the most dominating starting pitchers and fearsome power hitters in the major leagues.

But once again, the Giants turned the baseball world

on its head. They didn't just tame the Tigers—they mauled them. They swept Detroit in four straight games, including two back-to-back shutouts. And at the end of three crazy weeks in October, the never-say-die San Francisco Giants were World Series Champions once again.

So how did the Giants do it? How did they come back from the brink, over and over and over again?

The answer has everything to do with the players who surrounded Hunter Pence in the dugout huddle, who shared his passion and his intensity and his love for the game of baseball. Each and every one of them played an essential role in helping the team reach its ultimate goal.

Mister Perfect

Back in June, starting pitcher Matt Cain had etched his name into the record books when he pitched a perfect game—something no Giants pitcher had ever done before in the team's 130-year history.

On that magical night in San Francisco, the unflappable Cain set down all 27 batters he faced, allowing no hits and no walks. It was an electrifying game that had everyone at the ballpark holding their breath on every pitch. As it turned out, the joyous celebration after Cain's masterpiece was a preview of even greater things to come.

For although Cain was not perfect in the postseason, he started in all three of the team's series-clinching victories and was a calm and stable force in every game he pitched. He picked up his second World Series ring and cemented his reputation as one of baseball's best big-game performers.

The Comeback Kid

Behind the plate for Cain's "perfecto" and throughout the playoffs was 25-year-old catcher Buster Posey, whose sensational rookie season in 2010 had lifted the Giants to their first championship. But after that promising debut, Posey had to miss almost all of 2011 when his ankle was shattered in a gruesome collision at the plate. Some players never recover from that kind of injury.

Posey, however, rebounded with an awe-inspiring year in 2012. He started in the All-Star Game, won the major league batting title with a .336 average, and was named both Most Valuable Player and Comeback Player of the Year in the National League.

Buster put an exclamation point on his incredible season in Game 5 of the NLDS against the Reds. Until that point, Posey had not been hitting well in the postseason. But when he came to the plate with the bases loaded in the fifth inning, Buster blasted a monstrous grand-slam home run to left field. The ball was hit so hard that Reds pitcher Mat Latos didn't even bother to look up as it sailed into the second deck. That blow silenced the raucous crowd in Cincinnati and ultimately carried the Giants on to the League Championship.

Panda Power

After riding the bench for much of the 2010 World Series, Giants third baseman Pablo Sandoval had continued to struggle with his weight and injuries. But the fun-loving, free-swinging, bubblegum-popping "Kung Fu Panda" regained his power just in time for the 2012 playoffs.

Then, in the first game of the World Series, Sandoval had a truly historic night. On baseball's biggest stage, facing Detroit's finest pitchers, Sandoval clobbered not one, not two, but *three* mighty home runs!

As yet another Panda blast cleared the fence, television cameras caught Tiger All-Star hurler Justin Verlander quietly saying, "Wow." He spoke for baseball fans everywhere. In all of World Series history, only Babe Ruth, Reggie Jackson, and Albert Pujols had ever hit three homers in a single game before.

"Man, I still can't believe it," said Sandoval afterwards. "It's the game of your dreams. You don't want to wake up."

Scutaro's Revenge

When 36-year-old infielder Marco Scutaro was quietly traded from the Rockies to the Giants in July, it hardly seemed to be a blockbuster deal. After he took over the starting job at second base, however, Scutaro's unique combination of sparkling defense, clutch hitting, and veteran leadership provided just the spark the Giants needed to get to the postseason.

Scutaro proved just how much he meant to his new team in Game 2 of the NLCS against the Cardinals. In the top of the first inning, Cardinals baserunner Matt Holliday barreled into second base to break up a double play. The hulking Holliday, a former college football player, knocked Scutaro's legs out from under him and rolled over onto his ankle and knee. Marco writhed on the ground in pain for a few scary moments. Then he slowly, gingerly, got back on his feet and dusted himself off.

While the rest of the Giants fumed about the late slide, Scutaro took the high road. He accepted

Holliday's apology and stayed in the game.

But he did get his revenge.

Just three innings later, with the bases loaded, Scutaro lined a single to left field—right at Matt Holliday. Holliday fumbled the ball and watched it dribble through his legs. That error allowed three runs to score and gave the Giants plenty of cushion in a 7-1 victory.

Scutaro was named MVP for the NLCS and went on to knock in the World Series-winning run with two outs in the 10th inning of Game 4 against Detroit.

As it turned out, Scutaro lived up to his new nickname: "Blockbuster!"

Pitching In

Nobody symbolized the fighting spirit of the 2012 Giants more than the pitching staff, which was stacked with special players who had learned from experience to never give up.

In 2010, Barry Zito's once-stellar career had hit rock bottom when he was left off the Giants' playoff roster. But Zito endured that humiliation and worked his way back into the starting rotation. He then redeemed himself in 2012 with two of the biggest games of his career: a nearly flawless performance in Game 5 against

St. Louis and another solid victory in Game 1 of the World Series.

Meanwhile, journeyman pitcher Ryan Vogelsong had bounced around 15 different major and minor league teams over his 14-year career. He even played in Japan and Venezuela, but he never gave up on his major league dreams. "Vogey" finally found success as a starter in San Francisco, and he made the most of his first-ever trip to the postseason. He didn't allow more than one run in any of his four starts, and he tossed a shutout victory in Game 3 against Detroit.

Following that game, Vogelsong told reporters, "It's my first World Series. I've been waiting for this since I was five years old, and I wasn't going to go down without a fight, that's for sure."

Even Tim Lincecum, who had struggled through an absolutely awful 2012 season as a starter, became a powerful weapon for the Giants in the playoffs. When manager Bruce Bochy decided to use him as a relief pitcher, Lincecum never complained about his new role. In fact, he relished it. And whenever "The Freak" raced in from the bullpen during critical game situations, he delivered. Lincecum was practically unhittable as a postseason reliever, allowing just 3 hits and striking out 17 batters over 13 innings of work.

Twenty-Five Men. One Team.

All of these remarkable players had starring roles in the Giants' dramatic championship run. But the 2012 World Series victory was truly a team effort that involved everyone in the Giants organization, from top to bottom.

San Francisco's lineup in 2012 included several young "homegrown" players who played well under pressure, like shortstop Brandon Crawford, first baseman Brandon Belt, and starting pitcher Madison Bumgarner. Outfielders Angel Pagan and Gregor Blanco made outstanding catches and came through with timely hits throughout the playoffs. The bullpen, led by feisty closer Sergio Romo, shut down the big bats of opposing teams when games were on the line.

And, of course, there was twitchy, fidgety Hunter Pence himself. Throughout most of the postseason, Pence's on-field play hadn't quite lived up to the fire and brimstone of his inspirational pre-game sermons.

But in the third inning of Game 7 of the NLCS against St. Louis, Pence stepped up to bat with the bases loaded, no outs, and the Giants leading 2-0. While the Cardinals brought in a relief pitcher from the bullpen, the orange-and-black-clad San Francisco fans joyously sang along with Bon Jovi's "Living on a

Prayer." It looked like the perfect chance for Reverend Pence to blow the game wide open.

On the very first pitch, Pence took a vicious hack at an inside fastball, instantly shattering the handle of his bat. His sharp grounder bounced in the direction of the Cardinals shortstop, who broke to his right to field what appeared to be a routine double-play ball. But then the ball darted freakishly to his left and squirted into the outfield!

Scutaro, Sandoval, and Posey all scored on the play, and Pence ended up at second while the fans erupted in celebration. But what had just happened? Had the ball magically changed direction?

Slow-motion television replays told the rest of the story. As Pence was finishing his swing, the end of the broken bat somehow struck the ball a second time, and then, incredibly, a third time, giving it a strange sideways spin. Hunter Pence had catapulted the Giants into the World Series with one of the most bizarre broken-bat doubles in baseball history.

So that's how the Giants did it.

With a little bit of weird luck and a whole lot of heart, they played for each other and refused to give up. They ignored the immense pressure and just had fun playing a game they had all loved since they were kids.

When a team truly comes together like that, anything is possible. It's an amazing thing to see, and a lot of fun to be a part of. It's something the 2012 World Champion San Francisco Giants and their fans will never forget.